STARTUPLAND

Madness, Brilliance and PR Misadventures

Tales and travails of technology startups,
from two PR flacks.

*"In Startupland, survival is a reality show that
plays out every day."*

--Kevin Wolf

KEVIN WOLF AND POLLY TRAYLOR

ISBN: 1544074891
ISBN 13: 9781544074894

TABLE OF CONTENTS

FOREWORD

Tech Startups and PR: A Crucial Alliance

High-tech startups breed millionaires and sometimes billionaires. These scrappy, by-the-bootstraps operations are the ultimate symbol of American entrepreneurialism. Silicon Valley still holds a glimmering position as the ultimate place to live and work if you are in the software business, and most of the companies there today began as startups. CEOs at public tech companies are global celebrities – if not veritable heroes.

Yet working for a startup is tough; sometimes it's downright brutal. A software startup is the white-collar version of a sweatshop. Hang on tight, because the ride is bumpy and long, and words of comfort and praise are few and far between. As PR and marketing consultants to early-stage software firms, we get a unique, inside/outside view of Startupland. We represent the external view of the company to the public, portraying as best we can its shining moments of brilliance. We also see the inside view – both the chaos and the unbridled optimism.

We see errors in judgment, failures to delegate, raging egos, deadbeats, backstabbers, sudden cost-cutting, confusion and finger-pointing. We also see rapid development, admirable leadership, true teamwork, commitment and thoughtfulness.

The work we do is highly visible, which sometimes means we have to cover up the messes our clients make. Other times we share in the client's anger and disappointment when a valuable piece of news or stellar CEO interview doesn't make it to ink.

We have seen some clients succeed wildly in their market, and many others fail. Others, destined for mediocrity, may limp along with average results but with still enough revenue to maintain a small staff of loyalists. In few cases, startups can grow steadily and predictably. This is a black-and-white world of fundraising, furious coding, positioning and repositioning and of course, frequent staff turnovers.

Through it all, these upstarts continue raising money. There's a seemingly endless supply of money. But even having access to millions of venture capital dollars doesn't mean your path will be golden. We wrote this book to share our experiences and advice on PR strategies for a technology startup. We didn't want to write a manual of do's and don'ts – even though we include some here and there.

Instead, we chose to write stories about working with many different clients over the years. In the chapters that follow, we chronicle how they succeeded in PR and how and why they failed. Public relations, of course, is not a science. We can't snap our fingers and make somebody write a story.

There is no magic formula. We don't always understand why pitches fail or why reporters who cover a client's space regularly don't care about our client. It's a don't ask, don't tell environment.

Yet we do know that PR is extremely important for young startups – our clients tell us so, regularly. When you're getting going, with few customers and a beta product, you need the market to know who you are and to get ready for your next steps. Investing in PR to educate potential buyers, users and analysts on the company and its product is the best way to build awareness in the early days – and beyond. Certainly, the CEO and founders' business development efforts are crucial, but PR can be the right-hand man.

We know a lot about PR – Kevin has large agency and corporate PR experience before founding TPGR. Polly's 13 years of tech PR and marketing experience were preceded by several years in tech journalism. Yet we also know something about starting a tech company as well.

Kevin went through his own version of startup chaos when he invited two colleagues to join him in launching a site for software reviews. This was in 2006, when Silicon Valley had recovered somewhat from the dot-com crash of 1999 – and before the financial markets crash of 2008. It was a golden, albeit tempered time for startups, and Kevin wanted to make his mark.

The fashion at the time was for people to vote up or down a product, like Digg used to do for journalism. On the reviews site, products with the most "up" reviews would rise to the top of their categories. Vendors could pay to own and populate their pages, like Yelp does. There were no plans to allow more traditional advertising on the site. The idea was cool, fun and smart.

Yet early on, Kevin and his two business partners, women he'd met through other work, began to experience friction. It started when they made the snap decision to share the leadership role equally among them. They'd figure out job responsibilities later. The three amigos were on their way, and they did it right, with a Palo Alto attorney drafting up the paperwork and offering up some fancy office space to boot. "We felt like big shots," Kevin recalls.

Over the next several months, the trio developed the business and hired developers, including a group in India. They worked doggedly on branding, site designs, business plans and sales and marketing concepts. The team met two or three times a week and invested countless hours besides that, with no pay. The attorney created a stock plan and the trio began doling out shares to each other and third-party contractors and advisors. The business was coming together.

Shortly before they were ready to start sharing an alpha version of the site with friends and family, one of the partners brought up the issue of management. Specifically, she wanted to discuss who would be CEO of the venture. This partner was the most seasoned startup exec, having been a vice president of product and sales in at least two other startups, one of which had sold to Salesforce.com. In a somewhat contentious meeting, Kevin's two partners voted for the former VP partner to be CEO. He disagreed, because the business idea and vision had been his, originally. Yet since they owned two-thirds of the company, Kevin was outvoted and outnumbered.

Now the two had control of the company and they wielded that control like a big stick. In subsequent company meetings, Kevin's ideas were always shot down and often without much consideration. The energy had shifted—away from Kevin.

On a Saturday morning less than a year after Kevin had conceived the company, the partners called to say that they were "moving on" without him. He was contacted by their attorney to discuss the details. Kevin never spoke to his former partners again. Eventually, the idea and company withered away.

While this book is about PR, it's also a story about people. The best of innovations can be killed by a toxic culture or a self-absorbed CEO. By the same token, mediocre products sometimes result in big buyouts and investor love, thanks to the savvy strategies and winning personalities of those at the helm.

As external PR pros, we see some of the strange inner workings which others don't see. We see a lot of the warts that appear during stressful times. Dysfunction comes out in plain relief. There are pearls of wisdom too, such as the time when our client said, "Change is the only constant," when referring to tech startups. These moments show us how startups can succeed beyond all expectation simply by having reasonable, well-mannered leaders in charge and a smart, well-crafted strategy that isn't clouded by ego and overstepping.

All of our stories are real, though we've hidden names and details that would compromise the privacy of current and past clients. You may see glimmers of your own company in here and smile, and you may disagree with our analysis of what went wrong, or right. We hope you enjoy our insights into the nutty and fabulous world of high tech Startupland.

CHAPTER 1

THE LURE OF THE EXIT

The inception of most small businesses often begins with a dream… to stop working for someone else, to be your own boss, to do that thing you love instead of what you've been doing to make a buck. It's the dream of being beholden to no one but yourself, the promise that doing what you love will make work feel a little less like work.

This motivation, and not the drive to be a pioneer or rich beyond your wildest dreams, drives most small business owners to launch a company.

That's not at all how it is in Startupland, at least not for most entrepreneurs. Most startup founders begin with the end in sight: big returns from an IPO, merger or sale. Even since the recession of 2009, there have been some whopper exits: Zynga's 2011 IPO raised $1 billion, Twitter's IPO in 2013 rang in $1.82 billion, and let's not forget Facebook's widely-criticized IPO bonanza of $16 billion in 2012.

Then there are the recent mega buyouts: Cisco's $3.7 billion acquisition of AppDynamics, and Facebook's $19 billion snap up of WhatsApp. In 2015, there were at least 20 buyouts worth $100 million or more. In tech, big deals still happen with regular frequency: why not go for the gold when launching your company? A founder's motivations and decisions around financing and exit strategies affect all employees – and of course, the PR and marketing strategy.

Seeking the podium

Most of us can probably name more tech CEOs (Steve Jobs, Mark Zuckerberg, Bill Gates, etc.) than non-tech Fortune 500 CEOs or members of Congress. One client many years ago famously said: "Our product is going to be bigger than the Internet!" Even then, when the Internet still had unknown potential, it was a ludicrous statement.

Entrepreneurs often get caught up in their own creations, yet it's easy to surmise that this client coveted the perks, financial and personal, that would come with such an exit. His breathless enthusiasm, the gospel delivery... it all seemed to point to a breathless desire for fame.

If you live and breathe tech startups like we do, it's usually apparent from the first conversations with the founders where their true motivations lie. When discussing their market, product, competitors or predecessors, egoism often prevails: "There's nobody doing this today!" You can see the dollar signs spinning in their heads.

For PR people, that means you will likely spend a healthy portion of time talking the client off the cliff of PR disaster. Reporters see right through this hubris. PR pros know that the goal is to refocus that energy into useful discussions and storylines that will win credibility while still satisfying the founders' outsized ambitions.

Several years ago, we worked with a CEO who informed us early on that his mission was "to podium." By that he meant becoming one of the three most recognized and most successful companies in his space. This exec had a former career as a top guy in a software startup that had a great exit, as an IPO.

His company was part of a first wave of client server software and a segment of business software that was ahead of its time. The company wasn't the top player in the space, but they were up there – on the podium – and the return was nice.

In his new startup, he was sharp enough to see how the market was evolving. It was a busy space (financial software), with lots of new players and plenty of venture money and buzz. He had developed a strong product and was convinced it had the chops to succeed.

He also knew that having a really good product wouldn't be enough. He needed aggressive marketing and he wasn't afraid of being a little fast and loose with the facts.

You couldn't fault his thinking. Either he and his company were going to get out in front of the pack and be one of the few companies that industry leaders (and potential acquirers) would think of when reviewing the market landscape, or he was going to be left in the dust.

He knew the stakes from his last gig and he smelled another huge opportunity. This thinking and his strategy were evident the minute he explained his plan to podium. This wasn't the "just doing what I love" startup entrepreneur.

There are so many ways for a startup to fall short, and sometimes that reason is completely beyond the founders' control: lack of funding during a market downturn or dominance by a much larger and well-heeled competitor. Creating a company that can survive and carve out modest market share is in itself, a notable achievement in the cutthroat software sector.

Still, the exit beckons.

For PR people working with such a client, you've got to be aggressive in pulling out the stories that will interest reporters at business media outlets – the ones that investors read. That means asking the founder/CEO to give you human interest stories about their careers and adventures.

This can be tricky, if your CEO isn't a storyteller. You might have to sit him down over a beer or cocktail and work all the angles. The PR person's job is to find proof that the founder/CEO is the rock star she thinks she is: a leader who deserves money and market attention and who has experience making and selling great products that customers love.

Look for other opportunities as well to get the company in the limelight, such as lining up speaking gigs for the founders and execs at hot industry events, or encouraging the company to host their own meet and greets, where they invite high profile experts to speak.

Perception is critical here – but make sure to back it up with facts.

Making lemonade from lemons

We saw firsthand what a smart yet unknown client could do with a killer plan. Some years ago, we worked with a startup in the computer hardware market. They were based overseas and founded by a group of engineers.

The initial application of their technology was in the large-format display business, essentially making touch-screens for mall directories and digital signage. Signs and kiosks are not particularly exciting: but who knew then what would happen later with touchscreens. (The company launched well before the iPhone)

Shortly after founding they hired a CEO from a local investment firm: we'll call him Jim. He had been a top sales producer at a large computer manufacturer, but recently he'd been studying the touch industry.

Jim came to our client just before we signed on to work with them, and from our first interactions his plan for a positive exit was transparent.

The large-format display business that was the foundation of the company, the primary use of its technology and its major source of revenue, was doing fine. It was growing steadily, with clients and new orders coming in from around the world.

And then, in 2007, Apple launched the iPhone. Touch technology was capturing the attention of consumers and device manufacturers were anxious to capitalize. The world's largest desktop computer makers quickly began bringing products to market that incorporated touch.

Jim saw the writing on the wall: he and his company could keep developing touch solutions for large formats. They'd probably never get rich or become widely recognized outside their market segment, but the business would survive.

Their touch technology, which was different and more limited than the touch technology Apple was using in its products, would never be the market leader for consumer devices.

There was an alternative plan though. Our client could switch gears and target PC makers making touch-enabled desktop computers. The switch would require a complete re-imagining of the company, from product development to sales organization to marketing programs.

It would require support and resources from investors and understanding from customers who were buying their solutions for large-format applications and who would no longer be the company's main priority – even while they continued to be their primary source of revenue.

But that wasn't all the CEO needed. Every smart seller needs a buyer in mind. The CEO needed an exit strategy to ensure that when he got the company pivoted in the right direction, he could get out at just the proper moment.

PR to the rescue?
We were hired to execute the swing-for-the-fences strategy. The marketing exec was completely on board. He quickly put in place a two-pronged strategy.

First, we would position the company as a major player in the emerging touchscreen PC market. Next, we would aggressively tout any success in the touchscreen PC space. The marketing exec wanted to convey the message of: "We're the leader in this space."

We carried on, thinking there was more to the story than we had the privy of understanding.

During a six-month frenzy, we issued at least 10 press releases and made various bold claims to high-profile media including the *Wall Street Journal* and *USA Today*. We branched out, too.

With direction from the marketing director, we established relationships with PR teams in Taiwan, Japan and Korea, and began pursuing media coverage for the company's PC business in those markets.

This was no accident. The world's biggest computer manufacturers are based in Asia, and the CEO knew the importance of cementing those media relationships.

The company also began installing new leadership in Asia for the same reason, even though Asia was a relative afterthought for its large-format business.

In the background, our client was involved in a legal dispute with one of its competitors in the large-format industry. The competitor was suing them for patent infringement.

From our vantage point, we had no way of telling how things were playing out, since negotiations were happening behind the scenes with lawyers. What became clear to us later is that our client needed a parachute.

We had a nagging feeling (as did the media) that desktop touchscreen computers were not going be the next big thing in consumer electronics. We knew our client didn't have nearly as strong a position with PC makers as they would have liked. We knew that sales growth and marketing spend were starting to tighten up.

We guessed that the patent suit wouldn't go away quietly. Something had to give.

What happened next, ironically (or not) is our client was acquired by the company that was suing it. The purchase was to a) extend the buyer's reach into the large-format industry, b) expand its business into the PC industry, c) to give the buyer better geographical reach in Asia, and d) to end a costly patent dispute.

The marketing director seemed pleased if somewhat nervous about the transaction. The buyer had a successful large-format business already and didn't really need our client's customers or technology.

The PC business they were buying wasn't all we had cracked it up to be and the market for touch PCs was weak at best. And the patent situation: our client had far more to lose and would lose far more quickly than the buyer. Had the buyer waited another year, they probably could have bled our client dry.

It didn't take long for the transaction to sour. In the months after the deal was done, we never saw a single piece of good news reported by the buyer as it related to our former client.

There were no customer success stories, no related product developments and not even a quote we could uncover. Jim left soon thereafter – probably at the end of an earn-out period.

And then the crushing blow. The buyer was hit with a shareholder lawsuit related to our client's business. The complaint said that the buyer had made "material misstatements of fact" related to demand for its core products, including those it acquired from our client. It seemed as if our client had been inflating sales or potential sales.

To restate, startup founders often begin at the end, by charting a course to a successful exit and working backwards from there. Too often, the game plan reflects the process by which a company is funded.

When outside investors are involved, founders tend to follow a particular path. For our touchscreen CEO that meant: grow fast, give the appearance of being big and get out as soon as possible.

If the company relies heavily upon outside investors, PR people are at the whims of the get-rich, take-no-prisoners strategy. It takes an aggressive mindset and a thick skin to survive when the goals are so tied to an exit. Yet there is a silver lining: helping a client win big through smart PR and effective publicity in the right places can lead to new business with promising companies.

For podium CEOs who are looking for a fast path to riches and notoriety, the odds are slim and the journey will be rife with chaos. The podium CEO is less likely to make a lot of friends inside the company, unless he meets the goal and everyone gets richer and more famous, too. Working for a podium CEO means long hours, and sometimes impossible demands.

Not everyone can be a podium CEO nor work for one – it takes a certain temperament to embrace risk every day and pretend that work-life balance doesn't matter. The choice of taking on investors comes at a price, yet that reward can be worth the wait for one's pocketbook and career if the fast track leads to rapid marketplace success.

CHAPTER 2

The Self-Funded Startup

A startup's plans are different when the company is self-funded. The self-funded startup has more freedom and flexibility. A founder can build a company that emphasizes steady growth over risky acceleration, customer-driven product development over reactionary engineering, patient customer service over fire-drill support and profit over sales.

This approach doesn't mean that the founders don't care about a lucrative exit; it's just not the sole motivation for getting up every day. The self-funded startup can also be easier to support from a PR perspective, as there's more flexibility to tell a variety of stories, not just the ones indicating revenue growth and product releases. There tends to be more planning and less seat-of-the-pants reaction to the founder's idea of the next big thing.

One former client in the sales and marketing software space was founded by a serial entrepreneur and self-funded. All expenses, ranging from software development, sales and marketing to office space and furniture, landed squarely on the founder's credit card.

He had the freedom to grow at whatever pace he wanted, provided his bank account could support the trajectory.

He explained to us his game plan early on in the engagement. The company's top competitor, the industry leader, was an established public company; the runner-up in the space was also well known and had aligned with a key partner.

The third position was wide open: our client was focused on winning that spot. The goal was achievable and would earn the company a successful exit without requiring the kind of supercharged, burn-and-churn strategy that many startups undergo.

The founder's slow and steady business model manifested in many ways. For example, every quarter we announced their business results. We couldn't match the massive growth his competitors were announcing, so we focused on customer satisfaction.

Every vendor writes quotes for their customers to include in press releases, but our client's customer quotes were not mere spin. These were actual stories of happy customers using a product they genuinely loved. Imagine!

Bashing the competition is another tech industry trademark. Our client wanted no part of this game. We knew his competitors were constantly taking shots at his company and product and on more than one occasion, we advised our client to fight back.

He never did. Over and again he took the high road, choosing to let his product and customers do the talking.

He also created value for his business in the way he treated employees and vendors. It's common in Startupland for employees to move from one company to the next like frogs on lily pads.

Some of this has to do with landing bigger paychecks, but plenty of startup employees feel mistreated, burned out, disrespected, or under-appreciated: not at our client's company. In two years we never heard of a single person leaving.

On the contrary, the employees we encountered seemed genuinely happy to be there. It's not a stretch to say that being nice was part of our client's exit strategy, because, he posited, happy employees make better products and provide friendlier service.

All along, our client was steadily building a strong and appealing business. With our help, the company and product were now widely considered by analysts and press to be among the top three or four players in the space.

Unlike the number-two player in the category, our client had wisely taken the approach of building a product that worked well with many complementary systems. This was indicative of our client's slow-growth strategy.

It surely cost him dearly and took significant time to build integrations to many systems, but more integrations meant more potential buyers for his company.

Finally, the founder put his time and attention into PR and marketing. He knew the value of branding. He wasn't worried about taking time away from sales and operational duties to spend time with reporters, or write content that sold with editors.

This attention to detail around publicity is extremely rare. We knew we had a special client, and we also figured that somebody else with big pockets would take notice soon.

As expected, two years into our engagement with this startup, it was acquired by a larger firm. In typical fashion, there wasn't much hoopla, just a thank you note from the COO and the founder, acknowledging our contribution to their success.

The founder walked away with tens of millions of dollars. It was a huge win for a company of this size and a memorable example of a different way to achieve a successful exit. Nice guys don't always finish last, even in high tech.

Unlike the touchscreen CEO, the marketing software CEO wasn't interested in flash. There was no venture investment, sales at the expense of profits, growth at the expense of customer service, change at the expense of churn.

For this startup, slow and steady won the race: The classic tortoise and hare story.

Selling a company or going public can be a sensible plan from the start, yet getting there means making customers and employees and friendly contractors happy and building the business with enough time and planning to do it right. Funding, too, can make an enormous impact on the journey. Without investors breathing down one's back, there's little need to show off for the press, speak at every industry event or slam competitors to look smarter or bigger.

Bottom line, when deciding whether to seek outside funding or not, consider the consequences. Can you live with your decisions if the big exit never comes? Are you willing to endure the slow and steady ride? Can you live with being in the top 10 or 20 in your marketplace, and not in the top three? Is a steady paycheck and not a stock windfall enough to keep you and your team going? You can still have an exit strategy, on your own terms, and that may be worth all the potential financial sacrifices along the way.

If you can't build and grow your business without investors, then you'll have to make some choices for sure. Those choices involve the kind of people you hire and how you treat them, what goals you create and are they realistic, and if trampling over customers, competitors and partners is acceptable to get what you want.

As a PR team for a self-funded startup, there are distinct benefits from a measured approach to growth. Time and less pressure allow PR pros to build an arsenal of stories and long-term relationships with analysts and reporters. That can lead to the kind of coverage, profiles and features that launch a young executive's career.

For the self-funded startup, PR is just as important as the startup that depends upon outside investments. The self-funded startup may not have outside experts (such as VC partners) to help guide the company's hiring and go-to-market strategy. This can be freeing, but the startup still needs market support and awareness.

A creative PR team can help with those efforts, through traditional PR (news releases) as well as a variety of social PR strategies such as bylines, video segments on YouTube and blogs.

CHAPTER 3

DEATH BY INERTIA

What is it about highly-creative people that can make highly-organized people crazy?

For one, they can be scatter-brained. They love talking about new ideas, creating things and experimenting. Their minds catapult from one concept to the next.

They start on a project with full gusto, but before long, become distracted by something else shiny and new. This is not a negative personality trait. Yet it is an unpredictable work style, unlike a scientist who often approaches life and work in a linear, structured fashion.

Creative types are often the people who end up leading startups. The top engineers are (or should be) focused on product development. Marketing and PR consultants rarely work with the engineers; we work with the marketing directors, product managers and sometimes the CEOs directly.

This means, by default, learning to deal with constantly-changing expectations. The CEO in particular is pulled in too many directions in a small startup: product development, operations, marketing, investing, sales – everyone demands a piece of the chief.

The side effect is that progress can be slow on initiatives that are not directly related to creating and selling product.

It's common when we sign on with a new client to experience two initial weeks of flurried excitement. The client wants to create a media plan, ramp up the blog and write some articles. We respond in rapid fashion. Yet before long, the client inexplicably disappears.

They stop responding to emails to review content or schedule calls. They disagree with our edits on a press release, and go silent for days or even weeks. They eventually email that they will get back to us soon, pinky swear. Inertia sets in. Inertia is stifling and hard to turn around, especially for startup leaders who expect immediate results.

In PR, instant gratification is just not realistic for young companies with no name recognition – especially in sectors where there's already market saturation.

Of course, inertia is not just a problem in small companies and startups. Large companies can suffer terribly from inertia. That typically stems from too many people in duplicative roles, rigid processes and traditional ways of doing things rather than the chaos of a new company.

There's also the fact that at large companies, the threat of competition doesn't usually define every decision. In Startupland, survival is a reality show that plays out every day. So inertia, while sometimes related to the creative, unfocused and spirited nature of the startup's founders and early employees is also a product of stress.

The stress factor

In our personal lives, we all know firsthand the effect of high stress on decision-making. When an older relative or child is sick or a spouse loses his job, getting the simplest of things done can be a Herculean effort.

If the stressful phase continues for many months, inertia becomes a way of life. After a while, you fail to realize that you have started to live and operate quite differently. Inertia becomes the new normal.

Not all startups struggle with inertia. One company we worked with in the software development space was particularly good at balancing creativity and chaos with organized productivity.

The product executive whom we frequently worked with on projects was often on the road and had important leadership roles within the company, but somehow was able to keep up with our steady schedule of calls and content review.

The executive was not only highly intelligent and well spoken, but entirely pleasant each time we got him on the phone. He apologized profusely if he had to reschedule a call – even when the reason was absolutely justified, such as a last-minute investor meeting.

Does less inertia deliver faster growth? In the case of this client: yes. The software development company increased revenue 200% from Q2 2015 to Q2 2016, while signing multiple high-profile enterprise customers.

What's troubling about inertia in one area is that it likely signals inertia in other areas of the business: startup executives need to be able to complete tasks just like a mid-level manager in a larger company.

When a startup signs up for a new program – such as PR – but doesn't follow through, it makes one wonder if they're not following through on other issues, such as dealing with HR issues or facility needs.

Founders and CEOs with their heads in the right place are laser-focused on their customers, especially top customers. They calmly handle customer service issues or product bugs quickly and professionally.

When they're not doing that, they are selling and schmoozing partners and financiers. Of course customer care, sales and raising money are critical roles for startup execs. But as the company grows, the excuse of "things are just so crazy" begins to sound stale when other important tasks fall off track.

Executives who continue to overcommit, don't delegate well or staff appropriately, and can't properly see the big picture of everything a growing company needs to succeed are destined for failure.

Inertia: bad for branding

For marketers and PR people, inertia is an energy and momentum drain. The whole point of the practice is to create brand awareness in a respective market. If a company regularly disappears from the scene or decides to shut off funding periodically, the PR and marketing team must go underground, only to start over once the spigot turns back on.

That's a waste of effort, time and cash. The communicators and message makers can't get much traction in the marketplace through this inconsistent presence. They don't make meaningful connections with users and customers. They can't build synergies to help the company get to the next level.

Inertia creates inertia and nobody wins. For most startups, it's better not to invest in marketing, PR or other "extracurricular" activities until they are absolutely ready to devote the time on a regular basis.

Is there anything that can be done about inertia within a startup? Maybe. Sometimes inertia is a cultural trait that needs to be rooted out and dispelled by the CEO.

It could be that employees are stretched between too many projects and initiatives – and thus the CEO and other top execs should help prioritize goals and focus the team. Team bonding events or retreats are especially critical in small companies where people are under tight deadlines and must work at a high level of productivity all the time.

However, if the CEO is the one perpetrating this culture of inertia, that's another problem. People who are stuck in inertia may have had trouble making decisions or sticking to a plan for their entire lives. Completing something requires putting aside less important things, and for type-As, it can be hard if you want to do everything all at once.

Others, brought up by hard-charging (dare we say, helicopter) parents, can't begin to understand why someone wouldn't complete sometimes mundane tasks to achieve the bigger picture. And in high-tech PR, we understand that CEOs probably look at us as one more mundane task.

If we were hiring a CEO, we would look for the child of the strict, helicopter parent: The one who was always been held accountable for their promises and actions, who had to clean up their room every night before going out to play. The individual who didn't get to do every sport or after-school activity they desired as a kid probably learned to focus their energies on the things that they were allowed to do.

At some point in a startup's life, there are natural periods of inertia when founders and executives don't know the next step to take or when a marketplace barrier causes them to retrench. Yet, this should be a temporary place, not a normal mode of operation. When our clients succumb to inertia, we know that our time with them is growing short.

CHAPTER 4

LOVABLE LOSERS

Timing is to startups as location is to real estate. Of all the factors that can make or break your new tech company, from product design to marketing, when you launch and if the market is ready for your product are perhaps the most important indicators of whether you're going to succeed.

Startups with good timing are more likely to have a successful exit. Those that don't, in the tradition of startups that came before them, hang on until the money runs out.

The lovable loser phenomenon is one of our favorite startup stories. They're a dime a dozen in Silicon Valley. Streets from Mountain View to Palo Alto to San Francisco are literally paved with them. The dot-com boom gave us losers like Pets.com, Friendster, MySpace and WebVan: all good ideas with impeccably bad timing.

Poor timing isn't necessarily a case of misreading the market. Entrepreneurs and innovators will tell you that great ideas happen when they happen. Unfortunately, being first to market with a great idea doesn't guarantee you're going to end up the market leader.

Apple, for example, was not the first company to launch an MP3 player, smartphone or even a tablet. But they're a market leader in those categories now.

When nothing goes right

We worked with a company once that was ahead of its time. Based in Silicon Valley, the company was and is a provider of software delivered in the cloud model. It launched in 2000, before the term "cloud" was conceived.

The idea was to offer its software as a service, on a monthly basis, to small businesses. The Internet as we know it today was at the very earliest stages of adoption by corporate America. With millions of small businesses already paying for desktop software which constantly needed updating and maintenance, the notion of accessing the same tools over the web was nothing short of revolutionary.

The company subsequently developed what was by most accounts a very solid product. The original plan was to sell the product exclusively through a channel of resellers – which is how many small businesses buy software – but they soon switched to selling direct. The company had no trouble raising money from venture capitalists.

By 2001 they had raised over $30 million. The founders also had no trouble finding great talent to run the company. The first CEO was already known in the industry as a luminary and had been head of a software industry trade association.

By 2004, the company had roughly 1,000 customers. Revenues were still relatively small and the company was more than likely losing money, but business was otherwise strong. From a marketing perspective it was gaining a reputation as one of the first successful software-as-a-service vendors.

It was about that time that another startup launched a competitive product. The CEO of the rival company was a former Oracle executive. The company launched with funding from none other than Larry Ellison. Almost immediately, the rival began stealing some of our client's industry thunder.

No longer was our client the cool new toy; that domain now belonged to the rival.

The rival seemed to have an aptitude for flair. Their press announcements and coverage were stronger than ours, and their CEO was more press-friendly than his counterpart at our client company. By 2006, the rival had eclipsed our client in customers.

Meanwhile, our client began flailing. The original CEO had left the company and the replacement CEO was on his way out. A new CEO then joined to lead the business and initially he seemed like a winning choice.

He had been a top executive at IBM for many years and a confidant of Lou Gerstner. He had a "Relax, I know how to make this go" attitude, and he soon got the attention of press, customers and investors.

He launched new sales and marketing strategies; he launched a new customer service program built around total customer satisfaction; he raised an additional $36 million in venture financing from some of Silicon Valley's top firms.

Perhaps most importantly, he wasn't afraid to challenge our rival.

Over time, however, the momentum slowed and our client once again found itself in a rut. Product development seemed to lag months (if not more) behind its competitor.

The rival continued to make ever bolder statements about its place in the market, attacking larger customer opportunities, positioning itself against heavyweights like SAP rather than us, and generally beating our client to every punch. The rival company had raised tens of millions of dollars and was clearly getting ready for an IPO.

In 2009 and sitting on about 3,000 customers, our client's CEO was apparently pushed out by the board of directors. It was not clear to us, from the outside, why exactly this happened.

We heard rumors that his style, which could be considered gruff, rubbed some people the wrong the way. Now our client was going on its fourth CEO in six years. It was obvious to anyone watching from the outside that the company was in limbo.

Still, the company managed to raise yet more money (an additional $143 million between August 2010 and May 2016). It's anyone's guess where the money went. The new CEO had a much lighter, hands off style.

The company made attempts to expand its channel relationships and held annual, well-attended customer conferences. Product enhancements were still few and far between, but the company had a positive reputation with media and analysts.

Yet in 2007, the rival went public and the game was essentially over. The client, though to this day a respectable business, doesn't appear like it will ever get its day in the sun. Acquisition by a larger player seems likely.

Another possibility is that the client chugs along as a small company in a large market with no endpoint in sight.

Whatever the case, this client will be forever in our minds be a lovable loser: a company that, despite having a quality product in a big market, couldn't get over the hump. Whether for internal product development obstacles, poor direction, constantly changing management, lack of clarity on message or just plain bad luck, it seemed destined to be marginalized.

It appeared that the client lost to the rival because it was early to market with a SaaS product in a market that perhaps wasn't quite ready for SaaS. Their timing was off, maybe just by a year or two, but being second, as Apple has shown, has its benefits.

The rival seemed to learn from the client's mistakes in terms of channel or direct sales, messaging, speed of product development, and general aggressiveness in the market. Despite being first, our client was a step behind.

The lesson is that, even when you seem to be doing everything right, often times in the tech startup world, you fail anyway.

For the PR consultants, lovable losers are often wonderful clients – they're personable, have reasonable expectations and high ethics to boot. But those same qualities might just be part of the reason they fail: they lack the hard-to-handle tiger instincts which are needed to win.

CHAPTER 5

THE PROBLEM WITH PRESSURE

A famous song by legendary singer/songwriter Billy Joel starts like this: "You have to learn to pace yourself..Pressure. You're just like everybody else..Pressure. You've only had to run so far, so good. But you will come to a place where the only thing you feel are loaded guns in your face."

This emotion of "pressure" is all too familiar for the high-tech startup executive who works day and night to keep her company going in the right direction. She's got to please the board, keep employees productive and motivated and find new customers all the time.

Time frames in Startupland are as compressed as ever, making these challenges seem unmanageable even on a good day. Pressure and stress are necessary motivators, of course. While sometimes unpleasant, these emotions help us get a lot done in a short period of time. Pressure helps us strive for the best.

If you do PR for startups and can't handle the occasional off-mark comment in email or impatient tone during calls, perhaps this job is not for you.

When pressure gets out of hand though, the opposite can be true. The most capable of executives are those who can handle the pressure and keep their cool, even when the company might be in utter turmoil behind the scenes.

Turmoil isn't a necessary ingredient to create toxic stress in tech startups, especially in places like Silicon Valley, where competition is fierce and hubris is a common personality trait. Sometimes pressure is endemic to the culture. A CEO who can't handle pressure will negatively influence everyone else.

One exec, the CMO at one of our startup clients, frequently took digs at us and her direct reports on email. Early in the engagement with this company, "Linda" sent an email regarding an invoice.

Her remark was cutting: "Funny how the total is bang on the budget." During other exchanges, she would call out people on her own team with acerbic feedback such as: "That's a ridiculous premise. We would never speak on that topic. Totally off mark."

During calls, she was at times cordial and other times dismissive. It was hard to know what we'd get with Linda. Her company, a highly technical infrastructure software provider, was made up of primarily men.

Perhaps that male-dominant culture was affecting her demeanor, or maybe this was simply her nature?

Stress: we all have some control
Stress is unavoidable in life and particularly in fast-moving industries such as high tech. The trick is how to deal with

stress effectively so that it doesn't affect your interactions with others, your productivity, and your overall demeanor.

There have been numerous studies on the effect of stress on physical and mental health. A Yale study found that prolonged stress causes degeneration in the area of the brain responsible for self-control.

Research from the University of California, Berkeley, led by postdoctoral fellow Elizabeth Kirby, found that the onset of stress actually helps stimulate processes in the brain to improve memory. But when the stress is ongoing, forging into a prolonged state, the brain has impaired function in developing new cells.

In summary, these two studies suggest that stress is actually damaging to our brain, slowing us down, making us act erratically or anti-socially and even harming our memory.

One former client had an unusual communication style that bordered between passive aggressive and pitbull. On the first call with Kevin, "Sam" got irritated off the bat because he couldn't hear us clearly. Instead of trying to troubleshoot the problem, he gruffly blurted out: "We're going to have to get this figured out!"

That first call set the tone for the entire short-lived engagement. After a small communications gaffe, we received a tersely worded email listing all the things that we had supposedly (although not actually) done wrong in the past few weeks.

"I'm going to assume this is not indicative of the level of quality we should expect from your team and that we will see a marked improvement." It felt much like a reprimand from a middle school teacher, not a conversation between professionals working through a business relationship.

Bullies don't belong on the playground and they certainly don't belong in the world of startups. You ask, but what about Bill Gates? Steve Jobs? Larry Ellison? Aren't those some of the biggest bullies in the tech universe, people who have also been enormously successful in their careers, amassed incredible personal fortunes and made significant contributions to innovation and even important causes like world hunger and disease?

That's true, but let's be clear: these types of leaders come along once in a very long while. Like it or not, their collective impact on the high-tech industry and remarkable financial results in a weird way justified the narcissistic, irascible, untenable, bully behavior. Sorry Sam: you're not there yet.

Sam's startup operated in a highly competitive segment of web-based sales and marketing software. New companies were forming all the time, out of nowhere. There's got to be some pressure there, and this guy, who didn't exactly amass a Larry Ellison style fortune from previous startups, needed to deliver.

Unfortunately, the fact is, being the nice guy is somewhat irrelevant in cutthroat regions like Silicon Valley. A rough edge can help inspire the troops to deliver more, better, faster. Demanding the best possible results is part of being a leader, as long as you're willing to accept that you are in it with the team and not simply shouting orders down from the rafters.

Leaders who can roll up their sleeves and convey a positive, can-do attitude while still showing empathy are the type that startups need.

Managing stress is not something that the MBA schools typically teach. Corporate leaders rarely talk about it, especially in startups. There's plenty of advice on the topic, but some of it is just common sense. Get enough sleep, exercise most days of the week, eat well, don't drink too much, spend time with your family and friends, take up a hobby or passion no matter how small.

The best leaders are ones who don't or rarely show the stress or let it impair their work. If you ask them how they cope, it's likely they have a life outside of work and know how to relax doing something they enjoy on a regular basis.

Outside consultants may also be able to help with the stress factor. What can we do, as advisors, to take the stress off our clients? For one, always strive to be extremely easy to work with – be flexible on scheduling and ask for as little time as possible to get your work done.

Secondly, offer to take a task off the executive's plate – something that you could do just as well if not better. Thirdly, smile and stay calm when you're meeting with the stressed-out client. That positive attitude may rub off in positive ways.

These simple things could make the difference between a long-term relationship and one that ends after a month.

Regardless, there are some leaders who won't or can't change and they will never be able to prevent stress from having a negative influence on their business relationships. Look for the signs. You may not wish to do business with the individual who is a loaded cannon.

CHAPTER 6

INTERVIEW WITH JON HALLETT

We're lucky in that our line of work helping startups, we make friends with some bright and savvy executives. For this book we've chosen to interview a few of them, including Jon Hallett, who has helped fund a few of our clients.

Jon is Managing Director at Hallett Capital where he invests in and advises technology growth companies. Jon is currently serving as Chairman of the Board at BetterCloud and Salesfusion, as well as Board Director at Terminus, Rachio, MessageGears, Haste and several others. We picked his brain on a few startup topics from his many years of experience in the trenches.

What criteria do you use when investing in a startup and has this changed over the past few years?

For me it hasn't changed really. If you are going to invest in early stage ventures, the top thing to look at is the team. Ideas are a dime a dozen. If you look at the journey of a company, it's never just one great big idea.

Ultimately, at pre-revenue stage it's about the traits and personality of the team. It's also not just about the CEO, but the dynamic between people. A (Mark) Zuckerberg might need a (Sheryl) Sandberg, Jobs needed a Tim Cook. And there is no "model" CEO, either. You can have a techie CEO as long as he is complemented by the right person.

Some companies need more of an execution-focused operator and others might benefit most from a product innovator, and that depends on the stage of the company. After doing this for many years, I will say that there are a lot of nuances that come to play regarding matching the team to the opportunity. It's making sure you have the right people for the particular mission.

What are some red flags that turn you away from investing in a company or otherwise helping them?

This may seem obvious but self-awareness and integrity are critical. CEOs who oversell are a red flag. I want a realistic CEO who sees the challenges and worries and has a plan to tackle them. I look for pragmatists. If you are overly promotional it's usually born of insecurity or lack of substance.

Anyone who is not insanely passionate and committed to what they are trying to do will have a tough time succeeding. Building a startup is very difficult. It's 24/7. Also, if the CEO is drawing a high salary ahead of funding, that makes me nervous. Inherent in any startup is a risk-reward element and the best people are those who use early capital to hire other people versus paying themselves too much at the start.

At what stage should companies consider formal PR and marketing?

It depends on the capabilities of the team. There are two things startups need to do. They need to build the product and solve sales/distribution. Too many startups only focus on the product. I would bet on an inferior product with a great sales and marketing strategy over a superior product with a poor sales and marketing strategy.

Most techie startup executives find that appalling and would like the best product to always win, but that isn't the case. So you need a complete distribution strategy as early as possible. As soon as I begin the sales and marketing planning I would look at PR. This should happen very early on at least at a strategic level and even before the product is ready. PR can be a very powerful tool if used effectively.

If you had to give a startup CEO just one piece of advice to make it past early-stage, what would it be?

Continue to build a great team and coach them to optimal performance. As you mature, you've got to make sure the team can evolve for the challenge at hand. Companies will hit growth inflection points whether that is in people or revenues. The best CEOs are constantly evolving the operating model at each stage of growth and part of that evolution requires maturing the org model to support it.

Any CEO who continues to try and do it all themselves or allows for mediocre performance, will have a mediocre company. You've got to move people into the right jobs or move them out. This isn't fun, and it's not easy, but it's necessary because it's too competitive out there.

As an investor, I provide strong counsel around getting the right people in the right roles. That means even replacing the CEO if the CEO isn't the right person for the current or pending stage of growth. In most board discussions, when something is not going well, it is often due to lack of execution, and therefore fixed through personnel changes, not strategy.

CHAPTER 7

THE REVOLVING DOOR STARTUP

Change is a fact of life in Startupland. Companies change their names and sometimes, overnight, slyly pivot from one market to another. People come and go.

Much of the time it's necessary – especially in the early days of a company's founding. In tech, change can occur when a competitor or other mover/shaker disrupts the market. For PR, this is table stakes. Yet when change becomes the norm, the PR strategy is less sticky. It requires some tactical advice on brand consistency and messaging, and often that memo must go straight to the CEO. It's anyone's guess whether he or she will listen and adjust – and whether the PR firm will be able to hang with the chaos.

We've seen a few companies adapt to a market shift in technology, and that kind of change can be incredibly disruptive. Consider the touchscreen interface that's now mainstream in consumer computing devices. Touch screens were invented in the 1960s, and initially used in ATMs, kiosks and large displays, but it wasn't until Apple released the first version of its iPhone in 2007 that the general population really took notice.

Soon after, touchscreens were a critical component of not only phones, but many consumer electronics such as PCs, gaming consoles and tablets.

Companies also change direction through maturation. Many times a company is founded by a really smart guy, a.k.a. "the smartest guy in the room," who, all too often, happens to be an engineer without much business experience.

His product is amazing and appears to solve a real world problem, but once investors and an experienced CEO get a look at it, they have different ideas for where it should go next.

This is all *de rigueur* for startup life. Entrepreneurs in Silicon Valley and regions like it are constantly reinventing themselves in one way or another. Napkin ideas morph several times, even over the course of months (a veritable lifetime in high tech) before a company with a solid idea is formed and has seed money in the bank.

When change gets irrational

But sometimes, change is instituted when executives don't know what else to do amid troubling times – when the product they're selling isn't gaining traction or when it simply isn't working.

It may be cheaper or easier to move away from something than to fix it. The long and messy tale of Palm Inc. ended this way, after HP spent $1 billion buying the mobile device and OS company in 2010 and by 2012, had nearly killed it. The story of Palm finally ended in early 2014 when Qualcomm bought its remaining patents from HP.

So goes the glimmering world of high-tech, in which startups are darlings one day, and the next, are hastily tossed aside for something brighter. Palm and its failings have been overanalyzed in the media, yet the lesson is clear: execute or get out of the way.

Given the furious pace of change in startup breeding grounds like Silicon Valley, Austin and Manhattan, there's an unspoken yet widely shared sentiment that if you're not changing, you're not growing.

Unfortunately, this mindset can become a cyclical mode of operation that indicates a deeper problem. When too much change occurs in seemingly random ways, a startup is not growing, it's vacillating; senior managers don't know what to do next or can't smell the coffee that the great idea or product they hatched isn't resonating in the market.

In PR, we're often exposed to this "change addiction" when clients have frequent, unexplainable shifts in marketing messages, stories and goals. Positioning flip-flop is not all bad. It may be necessary when a competitor has usurped the messaging or a prominent analyst starts calling your market something else.

But when marketing plans change course quarterly, that's usually a sign that upper management has gone awry.

One company we worked with in a highly technical space became a victim of its own propensity for constant change: in product strategy, messaging and people.

The company's CEO was a likable sort of fellow from the get-go. He didn't seem caught up in typical startup ego, despite having had a very successful career already. In fact, he eschewed any of our attempts to position him as a thought leader. He was intelligent, well spoken, and approachable during calls and meetings.

Yet for an executive, he had an unusual obsession with social media. In particular, he was a self-professed Twitter junkie, and loved the idea of being a techie "insider" on the web. Whereas in some companies, a CEO's social media flair would be an advantage, in this case, it was a huge distraction. (We didn't say Donald Trump.)

His desire to keep up the Twitter buzz and connect with a few of his favorite techie bloggers was much stronger than his desire to work with us on a well-rounded PR program. Still, the relationship started off with promise.

Despite the CEO's quirks, he was pleasant and had a team of brainy engineers working on a software product that addressed a growing problem for IT departments turning to the cloud.

The problem soon became clear, however: Mr. Twitter was a control freak. He was never quite happy with whatever messages and strategy his internal team devised. Every few months, a new tagline appeared on the website along with a report from a prominent analyst describing such trend.

It was confusing and at times a hassle to re-educate the media as to what the company was talking about now.

Beyond the messaging madness, Mr. Twitter's perfectionism and indecisiveness were beginning to rear an ugly head of incompetence. These traits, we can only guess, led to serial turnover in the ranks.

The marketing director in charge when we were first hired by the startup had just completed a successful product launch. Mr. Twitter, exhibiting a personality trait that we later learned was typical, waited until the last minute to make massive and unnecessary changes to the press release.

The marketing director had been working 12-hour days updating the website and other content. The launch had been a great success, resulting in ample press coverage and some healthy leads to the sales team.

Inexplicably, Mr. Twitter called the marketing director into his office and said: "Congratulations. Great work on the launch. Now, I love the work you did, but I'll understand if you want to find another job."

The marketing director was naturally shocked and confused by the response, as anyone would be. He eventually left the company.

This pattern of smart people leaving the company seemed to continue at a regular cadence. We were sometimes entertained by the way staffers left: they simply disappeared. One day, a manager was helping us on a press release or bylined article. The next we'd be talking to the marketing director and the manager's name would come up.

We might ask, "Do you know when so-and-so is going to review that article we were working on?" To which he replied, "Oh that guy's gone now." It was like a scene out of

The Godfather. Without missing a beat, the marketing director continued, "Anyway, how about that press release?"

Did Mr. Twitter enjoy the continual replacement of his product managers and product marketers? There is a power in that, for sure. Yet constant turnover didn't help the CEO solve a fundamental problem: he didn't have a clear vision for the company and seemed to blame others for that. He was forever incapable of telling a coherent story.

Mr. Twitter wanted to stay inside the comfortable confines of the technology, where vision was less important than experimentation. Clearly, he liked engineers more than marketing and sales people, though he'd never admit that. He loved being The Boss. Yet a revolving door culture is toxic to a startup's longevity and credibility.

It became clear early on that Mr. Twitter generally hated making decisions and sticking with them. He didn't seem to care too much about getting press and often rebuffed our efforts to get his ideas into prominent business media outlets. He was most intrigued by jumping on the latest trend in his market, instead of deciding where his company fit best and what specific value it could deliver to customers.

Ultimately, Mr. Twitter left the startup – or was shown the door. Two years later, a much larger company acquired the product and the startup shut down.

The trickle-down effects of revolving doors
We've shown how a trigger-happy CEO (or other executive) causes lots of problems with strategy, positioning and staff morale. But there's more. When the lead marketer and

his team of product marketers changes, a company's positioning and/or how it sells its product is likely to change, too.

The change might be as subtle as a shift in pricing strategy, product name or website design. It can also mean a wholesale change in the market the company is targeting.

The company may have initially been targeting enterprise customers but then suddenly, they are selling to small and midsize businesses. At one startup, we worked with three different marketing directors over two and half years – and each one brought a radical shift in his own way.

The first guy was a seasoned startup marketer anxious to grab hold of the nearest industry trend. The second guy was hell-bent on content generation, and had us blogging until our fingers were blue. The third guy was a verbally abusive "interim" marketing director whom never worked to make a connection with us, or thoughtfully consider the best way to use PR to achieve his goals.

Dramatic shifts, even when positive, are hellish from a communications perspective. Imagine one day you're operating an ice cream truck selling Fudgesicles and Big Sticks, and the next day someone tells you that today you will be promoting Korean style pork burritos and chimichangas. You're not quite sure what people want in a burrito and how much they'll pay.

Even worse, kids in the neighborhood are going to be very confused. It will be easier for them to get their snack somewhere else, from someone else whom they know and trust to keep delivering the same delicious and reliable product.

Does the positioning run-around really matter? If a company has a fantastic product that people love, marketing and branding don't matter as much. If the company's minders are using different words and phrases here and there, and new people appear all the time, no big deal.

Even if they start introducing new products, they're still selling the one I like: no problem. Eventually, though, those chaotic internal workings will manifest themselves into a mediocre product or lower market share because no one knows what exactly you're selling today versus last week.

What we've learned is that startup executives should be flexible and open to change in the early days, but once a company's been established for a year or two and has a product in market, the knee-jerk culture needs to settle down.

Continuity of message, talent, culture and leadership become incredibly important. Innovation and predictability have to co-exist. Messages need to take root. Customers need to be convinced. Reporters need to be reminded. Staff needs the story to sink in and seep into the essence of the company.

If you think about it, good ideas take time to play out. There are plenty of overnight success stories, but most of the time, companies become strong over time. They may start with a groundbreaking idea, but execution, maturation and, most of all, stability are paramount.

That doesn't mean that a company won't have major transitions as it matures and grows, due to marketplace shifts, changes in customer demands or changes in technology. Yet after the change occurs, leaders should make every effort to return the company to stability and a steady trajectory.

Companies that are defined by constant change don't usually stick around for long.

CHAPTER 8

THE FUNNIEST STARTUP EXECUTIVE PERSONALITY TRAITS

We love startup founders: they're motivated, ambitious, a little crazy, usually very smart and sometimes just downright quirky. One can learn a lot about human nature – and your tolerance for its diversity – after working for many different startups. By no means an exhaustive list, we've compiled here a few of the more common startup executive personalities which we have encountered over the years.

Thank God you're here! Who are you again?
Startup execs are as demanding as they are busy. They know what they want and they want it now (if not sooner)! As a PR vendor, once hired you can expect to be thrown right into the fire… and sometimes under the bus. Beware the startup exec who can't wait for your guidance, only to completely disregard it and you.

The media kingmaker

These execs want to take credit for everything: the setting sun, flowers blooming, etc. We've run across one or two who are absolutely certain that the stories they pitched to reporters were so important, that they caused the reporters to be promoted or hired for new jobs. If you believe that line of garbage, I've got some swamp land in Florida to sell you.

But I want to be in the Wall Street Journal!

One of our favorite personalities is the exec who acts like a child. We run across these folks all the time and the trait often manifests itself when press coverage is being discussed. There's something about raising tens of millions of dollars in venture capital that makes an exec feel deserving of special attention from media. But here's a tip: Just because you *want* to be in the *Wall Street Journal*, doesn't mean you should be.

Here are the keys to the PR program, let me know how it turns out

This may seem like a positive personality trait but really it isn't. The best PR programs are partnerships in which each side, the client and the vendor, attempts to outwork/outservice the other. When execs hire us and then disappear, the PR program inevitably fails.

I don't think that comma belongs there

You're the CEO of an early stage startup. You've raised millions of dollars. You're hiring dozens of employees, many of whom have families that depend on your company to survive.

So, what in the world are you doing wordsmithing press re-leases?! First of all, you're a CEO, not a copy editor, so you probably have no idea what you're talking about. Second, get back to work on the important stuff.

I'm already rich so who cares

One exec we worked with was literally too rich to shake your hand. He'd made his tech money years ago and his new gig, as startup CEO, was his way of forcing people, whom he hired, to listen to his wacky ideas. Among them was the notion that somehow bumping elbows rather than shaking hands would "save your life." Or so he tried to convince us over a 6 a.m. breakfast at some unnecessarily expensive hotel.

I can't stop speaking in tech jargon

As PR people we're jaded when it comes to tech jargon. Sure, the occasional buzz word sometimes finds its way into one of our releases, but for the most part we understand that the press hate them, so we cut them out. But some startup execs just can't help themselves. They toss around tech jargon like frisbees. Seriously, what does it mean to "hypertarget" some-thing? And what the hell is "smart listening"? Give me a break.

I know we haven't spoken in a while but we need to issue that press release right now!

One minute you're planning a product launch, interacting with the client back and forth, and the next he or she stops responding entirely, for days or weeks at a time. Then, all of a sudden, you get a call or email saying "We have to issue that press release now!" Really? Where have you been for the last three weeks? And what happened to the plan we were discussing? These execs typically have a hard time delegating, which is why they've been ignoring your emails instead of asking their in-house marketing director to circle back with you on the product launch.

Dinner was great, thanks, but I don't want to pay for it

Every industry has its deadbeats and tech is no exception. We love the exec who has no problem asking you to do work but then is slow to pay or quick to question his or her invoice. Even better is the startup exec who cries poor, after he or she has used hours and hours of your time. Who goes to a restaurant and orders an expensive meal without money in his pocket? Some startup execs, apparently.

Passion for my company is literally oozing out of my pores

As a startup exec, if you're not passionate about your business, how can you possibly expect anyone else to be? While that's true, some execs take this too far. Passion tends to rub on off people in a good way, and if you're working long hours in a startup, there are worse things than a CEO who is constantly telling his employees that the work you're doing is changing the world. But like everything, moderation is important. Eventually, the overly passionate exec will not ring true.

You're the expert. How can I help you?

Hands down, this is our favorite startup exec personality type. The *How Can I Help You* exec is a rare breed but when you find one, hold on and never let go. These execs understand that their job is to hire the absolute best people, then offer to help them succeed. We've had the privilege of working with a few such startup execs over the years. They're almost always super secure with themselves, never feeling like they have to prove something. They're passionate without being irritating. They actually listen! Come to think of it, execs with this personality trait have led some of the most successful companies we've worked with in terms of how they exited. Who knows, maybe there's something to that?

CHAPTER 9

TIME TO GROW UP

Process is something that good managers bring to organizations. It comes from experience. Too often, startups ignore the fact that well-designed processes are an asset – and what a growing company desperately needs to avoid wasting time, losing money and looking incompetent with customers, partners and investors.

Of course, too much process is toxic to innovation and time-to-market: think Microsoft, HP, IBM and other Global 2000 technology companies.

Yet many startups seem to have a hard time growing up when the time is right. Even when the company is experiencing steady revenue growth, a staff of dozens and a growing customer base, leaders and founders can't break away from the notion that they're still in the basement drinking beer and throwing darts at the business plan.

Established companies post job ads like: "If you want to hang out with cool people, work hard and oh yeah, enjoy a cold brew while at the office, come join our team." It's interesting how the real trademarks of a successful company are hidden at the bottom of the posting: "401k, full benefits package and great opportunities for advancement."

News flash: employees of all ages want stability, a growth plan, recognition, and a company that knows how to operate professionally.

Surveys of IT workers continue to show that they crave the same fundamentals of workers in any sector: a competitive salary, a supportive work environment and community, and recognition. Fun perks like ping-pong tables, free food and dogs at work are nice, but certainly aren't a deal-breaker for any talented employee.

Here's the rub. Startups struggle to appease the Millennial generation, which values flexibility and a hands-off approach from the boss. Millennials are goal oriented and generally value collaboration with peers.

Yet in some cases, that Millennial culture can lead to a free-for-all environment where there aren't enough boundaries or, dare we say, rules.

Since we often work with early-stage startups, we see the painful results of the "process-lite" culture: micromanagement, high attrition, poor communications, no-shows at meetings, last-minute decisions and hopelessly late payments.

What's particularly shocking is that many of these tech startups are funded by VCs that employ seasoned executives who should be able to coach their clients on solid processes for meetings, communications, talent management and finances.

In many cases, the value of people working round-the-clock to develop the next Facebook or Uber, properly fueled with caffeinated beverages and snacks, seems to trump more traditional company values.

Some entrepreneurs believe that process is an innovation killer. Yet, we've also seen the opposite to be true. The company without adequate structure, leadership and oversight can quickly become mired in cycles of indecision and inefficiency.

Process starts at the top

Consultants such as ourselves love access to the CEO: these individuals often have the most invested in the success of the company and are closest to the customers. The CEO might even be the technology brainchild for the product or service and possess unique knowledge about the marketplace.

But when we start hearing too much from the CEO, we worry. When the CEO is line-editing articles and press releases, that can't be a good thing. When CEOs are sitting in on every PR call, including brainstorming meetings for story ideas, one begins to wonder who is meeting with the customers, partners, R&D team and investors?

Having the confidence to delegate day-to-day business activities to the people who own them (a.k.a. marketing staff) is a critical quality for any executive. In the cutthroat world of tech, the inability to let go is especially troubling.

One CEO with whom we worked insisted on being in on every planning meeting and frequently proceeded to haggle over messages and positioning with the CTO. Not only was this a waste of everyone's time, but it showed a consistent lack of agreement between the two top executives on what the company was doing and how it should communicate those ideas to the market.

We recently worked with a startup that repeatedly demonstrated a shockingly poor ability to lay out and follow simple processes, so much so that it made us wonder how on earth these guys stayed in business at all!

From the outside, this was a company doing everything right. They had raised money from prominent venture capitalists and hired top talent from the SaaS industry. Their team had developed an innovative product in the hot market of big data. They said all the right things about how they wanted to run the business: aggressive but smart, fast but with attention to detail, savvy but not too full of themselves.

We were brought in as PR counsel to help execute their content and media strategies. The client was attractive to us immediately because of our background helping companies in the IT management software space.

The VP of Marketing had also been a client previously. That said, we hadn't worked with this person long or closely. The VP, "Steve," was a nice guy: ambitious, logical, diplomatic. Steve also had a knack for jargon, meaning he used too much of it with comments like: "We're giving DevOps the stage by empowering them with insight."

He could tell a good story, or at least a story that sounded good, but it was hard to pin him down. Was his guidance on PR and marketing activities vague because he didn't know what he wanted, or was he simply a poor communicator?

It was Spring 2013 and our first assignment was announcing the firm's latest funding round. We moved quickly as the CEO was anxious to get the story out. We pitched a lot of reporters and delivered nice results for the client. It was the start of a good relationship and a strong PR program.

Soon after the funding release went live, we had a call with Steve to discuss next steps. We were adamant that PR was a process, not an event, and doing it right meant making a commitment to creating and pitching content on a regular basis.

This wasn't just some attempt to bill more hours and make more money; as we told him, whether we do it or you do it, PR is something that needs to happen every day, for as long as you're in business. He assured us this would be the case. We discussed a series of activities, ranging from customer stories to byline articles and blog posts.

Fast forward to Summer 2014 and almost none of those earlier goals had been achieved. Our client couldn't seem to keep things going on a regular basis. We'd start a press release and never issue it. We'd discuss the need for customer stories but they never materialized. We created a list of potential byline articles but the client never followed up.

Steve seemed to recognize the need for process but had trouble translating plans into actions.

It's extremely common for marketing execs in startups to behave this way. It's also understandable. They are some of the most overworked, underappreciated people in tech. When things are going well and their companies are making money, it's because the product and sales people are great. When the company falters, it's marketing's fault.

It wasn't as if our client didn't have a lot on his plate. He did. And it's not like he had a large team of people to help him execute things like finishing a press release or finding a customer reference. He didn't. It certainly wasn't because he wasn't smart or capable.

We were always impressed by his passion for his work and knowledge of the industry. He appeared to have the support of management, too. The CEO often deferred to his judgment, never pushing back too hard.

As it happened, Steve left the company in 2015, which soon ended our engagement with the client as well. He went on to take a job as CMO of an earlier stage startup. He lasted there less than a year and is now in Marketing at yet another startup.

Steve's strength was his ability to articulate a vision for a company or product. His weakness was an inability to put that vision into something tangible. Process to him became an enemy rather than any ally. In the end, he became the victim of his own big ideas.

Now for the good news: Smart processes are not impossible in Startupland, once a company decides it's time to begin acting like an established player. Four years ago, a client came to us with a challenge. The CEO said, "Our product captures a ton of data. How can we make use of that data to promote our business?"

The client had a straightforward goal, and he was asking for help defining and implementing a plan.

We quickly came up with the idea to aggregate and anonymize our client's data and release it quarterly as a report on the status of the business travel market (our client's industry). For several years, the story has been picked up by nearly every major U.S. news outlet, including CNN, NBC, USA Today, Wall Street Journal, New York Times and NPR.

Suffice to say, the client was quite pleased. And while we'd like to take full credit, in truth, much of the credit goes to the client. Unlike many CEOs with whom we deal, this client knew what he wanted, stated it clearly, and allowed us to craft and implement a strategy. And then, importantly, he stuck to the process.

It should be noted that we changed the process along the way to maximize results. About a year into this project, we tweaked the quarterly reports to include a new and very topical set of data. Using the new data, we were able to tap into a broader group of media.

The result was a substantial boost in press coverage, reminding us that even the best processes should be fluid.

Developing effective business processes for corporate communications, marketing and other functions doesn't have to be difficult. It takes commitment to operational tasks that may not seem fundamental to achieving the broader go-to-market plans.

Most startup leaders we work with express a desire to develop and implement process, but fall short on execution. That may have something to do with the pace (rapid) that most startup leaders maintain. The leader may lack an organizational or operational background. Whatever the case, process is paramount to startup success.

Companies that get this stand a better chance of finding and retaining top talent, delighting customers and forging long-standing, mutually satisfying vendor relationships. Companies that don't, well, they probably won't know until it's too late.

CHAPTER 10

INTERVIEW WITH MATT GERBER

Matt is CEO of Rohinni, a global leader in the use of micro-LEDs for lighting applications. Its clients are OEMs in consumer hardware, from wearables to PCs. Matt has served as CEO and/or board directors for several startups, including Digital Fortress, 2nd Watch, SprayCool and Blue Box Group.

You're a serial startup CEO. What are some important ways that a leader can help an early stage fly-by-night startup evolve to a more established and professional company?

Startups have to change the way they interact with prospects as they grow up. In the early stages, they are like the lion at the zoo. Everyone wants to look at it, but no one wants to get into the cage because it's too risky.

It's remarkable to see how much interaction with customers happens at startups, but there is very little business as a result. Almost anyone will talk to a startup about product.

They all want to learn. Big companies hire people to research the marketplace for acquisitions and new ideas. So you can easily waste your time.

The first step is to figure out which of those prospects will get into the cage with you. Therefore, you need to put people and processes in place to do the real prospecting and qualifying. Entrepreneurs hate to say no to meetings and calls. But you have got to be more selective about who you talk to.

Secondly is prioritization: what do you work on? With early stage startups, it's extremely prospect-driven. Once you have cleaned up the front end and are talking to the right people, then it's time to clean up the back end. Where do you focus development?

You always have too many things to work on and too few people. You bring the salespeople together with the engineering and production people, and look at the several possible new features to implement. You've got to pick which ones to do next – which ones are important for the top customers.

And that is where a good leader comes in to help guide the direction. That is also where you see most of the conflict. The founder's been focused on getting a deal done from the beginning, but that is sometimes counter to getting the right processes in place later on.

How can you balance innovation with process and operational excellence?

There can be process put around prioritizing what you need to do and determining what resources you have in place to get it done. If you have a company that is short on cash and needs to show a win in marketplace, the decision is obvious. It's about survival.

You work on three new features for three prospects in a month, versus working on the next gen of the tech that could change the world. However, if you have just gone through a round of funding, and you see an opportunity to change the world and you're getting good feedback from customers in that regard, then maybe you can look at the bigger picture.

You decide to spend 90% of your time on the next release of the product, over the next six months. You will not be driving revenue, but you will be perhaps changing the world. It is really situationally dependent.

Why and how is PR important at the early stage startup?

For an early stage company that needs funding, PR can be one of the most effective ways to get the word out to the marketplace. PR is extremely effective at generating market interest and good leads, compared with going to trade shows or buying online ads. PR reaches a broader audience.

When people who have read about your company on third-party sites take interest they already have some base knowledge about your offerings. They are already qualified. Even when the product hasn't been released yet, PR is valuable. With my current company, we've used PR effectively to tell the world we are out here, even though we don't have a product to market yet. It has helped validate a fit to market thesis for us, and that's led to investor interest.

Can you describe a difficult leadership situation and how you got through it?

The hardest one is as you try and introduce process, you have pockets of people, often the founder, who fundamentally disagree with the need for process and structure. With a first time entrepreneur there is always conflict as business scales, especially when an outside leader comes into the picture.

It's very much a case of needing to politick. You have to lead by example, show previous successes, prove yourself, and there is a lot of cajoling – eating and drinking with people. By doing all that, in many cases you can succeed. But sometimes the founder has to leave. They can't or don't want to make the transition.

People who are drawn to a pre-revenue startup are not always the same ones who want to sit through the four-hour engineering meeting discussing priorities. People who want to change the world may not want to be in the same environment as the company grows.

CHAPTER 11

WORKING WITH THE PRESS

There's no "formula" for working effectively with members of the media. Reporters and editors are as different as one's neighbors, with one exception: they generally don't trust PR people. If they do, they won't readily admit it.

The smart PR person takes his time to win the trust and respect of the writers and editors whom they are pitching. Yet sometimes, no matter what you do, journalists are still going to distrust you. But at least, if you do your job right, they will consider your pitch.

Curiously, this animosity hasn't always been the case, as Kevin shares from his early days working in PR. This was a virtual lifetime ago, mind you, around the time that Al Gore invented the Internet! (Ha ha)

Here below are Kevin's memories of "the good ole days" in the mid-90s. Computers were becoming mainstream in offices, and the days of interviewing story sources over a three-martini lunch were (pretty much) long gone. Reporters worked hard, probably harder than today, because they were still painstakingly flipping through paper files to research their stories and they couldn't Google a fact in ten seconds.

But the cool thing is, they answered the phone.

As Kevin shares:

Twenty years ago I was working for a small public relations firm in Silicon Valley that had big clients making semiconductors and other equipment in the still-nascent high-tech industry.

The founders, Bob and Frank, were expert strategists and Bob was a wonderful wordsmith. They got their start in PR doing publicity for Debbie Reynolds and other actresses in Hollywood in the 1950s. They were gay and the equivalent of married, and moved to the Bay Area together to deliver PR services to local tech companies.

I joined the company in 1995, right out of college. I'd never held a job in PR before and really had no idea what I was doing. Bob, Frank and a handful of other PR pros were the core team. Our main role was media liaison to a relatively small number of industry reporters and associated analysts.

The subject matter – semiconductor manufacturing equipment – was about as in the weeds as it gets from a technology standpoint. There were no slick mobile apps for us to pitch.

I learned the ropes mainly by watching and listening. Cliff and Patty, my direct bosses, taught me how to write a press release, create a media list, and pitch an editor. Cliff was more salesman than marketer. He was known in the office as the King of Analogies, because he could make a complex topic like photolithography easy to grasp for a layperson or novice, like myself.

He'd say something like, "So extreme ultraviolet lithography is like tracing someone's picture on a thumbnail size object under a very bright light." That sort of casual discourse made highly-complex products easier to understand and subsequently easier to explain to reporters.

My first time observing Cliff or Patty pitch a reporter was before a trade show. We were traveling to Asia for SEMICON Taiwan and wanted to schedule interviews for our clients with reporters attending the show.

At the time, in 1995, this was a totally achievable goal. In retrospect, this sounds ridiculous. Back then, if you wanted to meet a reporter and you had a client whose products fell into his beat, you simply called the reporter and asked for the meeting. You told him or her what you were calling about and why.

You explained that your client was announcing a new product and would be at the show. You asked for his availability and agreed on a location to meet. Once the logistics were ironed out, you hung up.

The 10-second analysis

Several things about that process don't apply today. For starters, you can no longer call a reporter. Most reporters don't even bother picking up the phone if they don't know the number of the person calling – and none of them know a PR person's number unless he's a relative. Back then, we also didn't have call waiting. Reporters were literally picking up the phone blindly (can you imagine?!), throwing editorial caution to the wind.

Nowadays we wouldn't *ask* a reporter for an interview. We would email, text, IM, tweet, DM, Snapchat or whatever form of online communication is available today. This supposedly far more efficient and non-invasive process really isn't any better – for anyone.

Before, it was a simple "Hello, this is Kevin, are you still going to SEMICON, and did you want to meet XYZ company about its new etching product?" The response was brief and cordial: "Sure, sounds good, how about 10am on Tuesday?"

Now, well, it's a different story. First you send the reporter an email. It's understood that the reporter won't reply, because she has already received 150 other pitches that day and is behind on a deadline, because her publication has cut back on staff due to the Internet's weak business model for making money in publishing.

After the reporter doesn't email you back, you, as the responsible PR person, must do the thankless job of emailing the reporter again. You might call them just for fun, but if they pick up and give you a minute, you better have the words smart and quick.

Either way, the PR person is just doing her job, bugging the reporter who is also just trying to do his job.

But wait. Most reporters have to think pretty hard to come up with the incredibly insightful stories to which we're now accustomed, the kind of stories that their editors are begging for because they need page views to get advertisers.

They do sometimes (maybe often) need a lead, a source, or a tip – so if there is an opening, it takes finesse to communicate your message in such a way that you won't be ignored.

Yet, it still comes down to luck: did you reach the reporter with the right message at the right time when she is in the right frame of mind to receive it and act? (If this sounds like yet another twist on personalized, real-time marketing, it is). If you spend too much time on anything, spend it on writing the pitch and the email subject line.

You've got to catch the reporter's attention quickly and clearly. This is the PR 3-second rule: you have three seconds or less to make an impact on a journalist. Otherwise, that handy delete button will kill your amazing, newsworthy pitch.

Perhaps the biggest difference between doing media relations then and now is that reporters today can simply and swiftly blow you off entirely. As I said, reporters 20 years ago actually had to speak to PR people.

If they didn't like your pitch, they had to tell you so because you had them on the phone. That takes nerve. Today, hiding behind electronic communications, reporters can ignore you quite easily. They ask for email interviews, if anything at all, because they (presumably) don't have time for a call.

That's nice for them, but it's made the job of PR a whole bunch tougher.

Let's stop for a moment to consider that we as PR people really do like reporters. In fact, many of us, like Polly, once held down jobs making decent money as journalists.

We respect their work, we like to read their work, and we think they are highly valuable members of the free world.

Yet like any reasonable human being, if we know that we are a good PR person – smart, ethical, helpful and respectful of time – we don't want to be treated like the discarded, greasy sandwich bag from lunch.

Deflect and ignore: the reality of online journalism

Covering Startupland as a reporter is like drinking from the firehouse, 24 hours a day. There are approximately 26,000 startups in Silicon Valley alone and thousands more in New York, Boston, Atlanta, Austin, Israel, London, Toronto, Seattle and so forth.

This makes a reporter's job a bear because they're overwhelmed by pitches. We know they can filter their inboxes with keyword searches. The smart and well-trained reporters know that 10 minutes on the phone with a source is better than 10 or 20 back-and-forth emails with a PR person, any day.

Many reporters have separate, private email accounts where they do most of their work, ignoring the corporate account unless absolutely desperate for a lead. So, while you're wondering if reporters are just plain lazy, consider this fact: the modern day reporter got screwed.

When the Internet came along, traditional media business models got smashed to hell. Many pubs perished but some survived, albeit with skeleton writing teams because ad dollars were too small to accommodate more than a few full-time journalists. The funny thing is, publishing companies of the time didn't get the memo right away.

Tech was booming in the late 1990s, and new magazines and websites were popping up all over the place to chronicle this bold new age. We were blessed with *The Industry Standard, Business 2.0, Upside* and *Red Herring.* These legendary publications flourished for about three years. When the ad money dried up, they withered and died.

When the pubs got smaller, the beats got larger and the pay went south. Journalists who used to cover financial software were now covering all kinds of software. I don't know where the Writer's Union was on this one, but you might as well have told a teacher he or she was about to go from teaching a class of a dozen or so kids to a class of 5,000.

This was too much for most writers (understandably so), so many just stopped responding to pitches. And those who did respond gave PR people an earful. The smart, well-known ones found high-paying jobs with Gartner, IDC, or other tech analyst firms.

Before the Internet blew up the publishing business, reporters and PR people treated each other with civility, not hostility. We didn't have agendas so much as we had shared objectives. There was mutual respect. There was a thing called courtesy.

You called someone on the phone when there was a reason, you didn't take more of their time than was necessary, and you exchanged meaningful pleasantries at the conclusion of said conversations. The result: professional stories by professional journalists.

Try humor?
Cliff (from Kevin's old PR firm) was better about interacting with reporters than any PR person Kevin has worked with

in more than 20 years. His style was comic confidence. He knew the subject matter, because he saw no reason to be ignorant or look foolish.

He was quick with a joke or analogy. He was charming and could make reporters and clients alike feel at ease.

Before sending Kevin to Asia for that trade show, Kevin listened while Cliff called reporters and booked meetings. He was on a first-name basis with all the major semiconductor reporters at the time, since reporters didn't switch jobs or beats every six months as they do now.

He could get them on the phone and have them up to speed on a new product within a few minutes. Two more and the meeting was booked, everyone on to the next thing. And then PR got complicated.

Adding to the mix: sky-high startup expectations

Nowadays, working with media isn't fast or collegial. It's arduous and uncomfortable and also mysterious and somewhat intoxicating. Startups today understand very well the value of media relations. Among marketing costs for B2B startups, it's no doubt a sizable one.

Startups covet coverage even though the financial return on coverage is hard to quantify. They understand its value as a branding exercise. They see how media are really just analysts, telling people what to buy.

Entrepreneurs want and need those endorsements, so they lavish money on PR firms and consultants and in-house teams. And they hatch strategies and reasons why their product is best and why reporters are going to be excited. And they teach the PR person to convey these messages. They ask questions about the process but most don't get too close to the fire.

They want coverage but most aren't sure where: just get them ink.

Most startup CEOs have a few media connections of their own. Their investors throw parties on roof decks in 75 degree Silicon Valley weather, which journalists attend, perhaps hoping for their own slice of billionaire pie, or at least a very good free drink. Startup CEOs engage and after a short time they exchange SnapChat or Instagram details.

Suddenly, the CEO understands tech PR.

One of our old clients was overly confident in his media skills. We were announcing the appointment of a debt funding round (essentially a loan that would likely never be paid back), and the CEO was, inexplicably, expecting coverage in the top tech media sites.

Here's reality: no unknown tech startup is getting coverage for a tiny debt funding. Any reporter who wrote this story would be laughed at by their colleagues for having so much as read the pitch. But pitch it we did.

Alas, we didn't immediately get the attention of a top tech journo (shocker!), and the CEO was miffed. He was particularly frustrated that we didn't check with him before doing outreach, so we could leverage his "connections." He knew so and so from TechCrunch or whatever and could have called him, which he eventually did.

Of course, the reporter blew him off.

And so it goes. We've worked with many clients however, who actually know how the game works. There was the COO of a marketing startup in the southeastern U.S. who didn't know how to lie. He was a martial arts student and had zero ego. When he talked to reporters, they listened, because there was substance, not fluff.

Another media expert client was CEO of a learning software company. She was easily more articulate, demanding, shrewd and personable than most male CEOs we've met. When it came to dealing with media, she was straightforward and calm, despite having a speech impediment that could have made her self-conscious.

She was an expert businesswoman and honest as the day is long. And when we worked with her on contributed articles, she was one of the few to provide thoughtful feedback and edits. The company she ran didn't have an exciting product, which limited its press opportunities. Nevertheless, she always spoke eloquently about her company and service, and her interactions with media were positive.

It's not a small thing to say that without media, there would be far fewer tech PR people. This is truly a relationship of need and survival.

But it's a fragile and often confrontational relationship. Tech PR people and press need each other like Democrats and Republicans, but they're just as likely to eat each other alive as hug at a venture capitalist cocktail party. It's a game we just keep on playing.

After all this, you might be thinking: never mind. This can't hardly be worth the effort! But wait a minute, there is hope. You can strive for decent media relations without burning bridges and tearing your hair out every night over the martini you wish you could have had at lunch.

CHAPTER 12

How to Make Technology Reporters and Editors Cringe

Tell them your product is the first of its kind on the market
Every product has a competitor, even if the competitor is a build-it-yourself product or manual process. Telling a reporter or editor your client's product is the only product of its kind on the market suggests you're either not that smart or you just don't have all the facts.

Refer to the reporter/editor as "sir" or "ma'am"
Nothing says "I'm a telemarketer!" like a Dear Sir/Ma'am intro. Reporters and editors are people, too. A sir or ma'am intro makes them feel like your pitch was sent by a computer instead of an actual person. Don't send mass-market emails. Tailor each email to the individual reporter, noting his/her name and beat or recent coverage that applies to your pitch.

Send an initial pitch that is more than two paragraphs

The top reporters and editors receive hundreds of pitches daily. In order to get any actual work done, they have about three seconds to review your pitch. Anything longer than two very short paragraphs is too much. A long email pitch may as well not have been sent at all.

Include multiple attachments in your initial pitch

Unsolicited attachments immediately strike fear into the hearts of recipients: Could this be a virus? Unless you've connected already and the reporter is expecting your attached press release, headshot, etc., don't send.

Send email asking if they got your previous email

If they didn't reply before, shoot a follow-up email a day or so later if you are highly confident the reporter is the ideal person to cover the news (use this tactic with caution). But don't ask if they got your first email. If they did and didn't respond it's because a) they're too busy or b) they're too busy and aren't interested. These days, with all of us on devices 24/7, trust me when I tell you they got your original message.

Send email asking when your article is going to run

This is a fair question to ask an editor, who frequently has a say about when something publishes. Never ask this question of a reporter, however. They don't know the answer and usually don't care. Their job is to write stories, not manage publishing schedules.

Send email asking for a non fact-based editorial correction
This is a big no-no. If the reporter misspelled your client's name or got the founding date wrong, go ahead and ask for a correction. If you don't like the way the reporter described your company or product, keep your mouth shut and look in the mirror: it was probably you (or your client) who could've done a better job describing it.

Cite your client as the "leading provider" in some technology category
Every tech company likes to say it's the leading provider of "whatever" but those claims are almost never backed up and reporters and editors know it. Trying to position your client as a leader without credible supporting data just annoys reporters and editors.

Use jargon in your pitch or press release
Journalists hate these buzzwords: "revolutionary, innovative, transformative, pioneering, game-changing..." Use straightforward language and keep it simple.

Write long, complicated, "insider" press releases
Get rid of the long-winded phrases and complex scientific terms. Write the release so that someone with zero background in your industry will get the jist quickly. The days of beat reporters are over; someone covering your story may be writing about five other sectors at the same time.

CHAPTER 13

You Can Trust Me

In the 1986 film, *"Hoosiers"*, the coach of a rural Indiana high school basketball team is a crusty, argumentative type (played aptly by Gene Hackman). Coach Dale, a man with a checkered past, has struggled to turn a small, unproven team into champions.

Miraculously, the team gets to the State championship game. During the final moments of the game, Dale gives instructions to his team on how to close the deal. When he asks one of the star players, "Jimmy," to pass but not shoot the ball, his teammates look crestfallen.

After a pregnant pause, Jimmy pipes up: "I can make it, Coach." Dale acquiesces and the underdogs go on to win the title through Jimmy's final courageous shot from mid-court.

That's trust: abandoning your pre-conceived notions and fears to allow someone else to take over. Startup founders and executives often struggle with trust. After all, it's been their blood, sweat and tears that have moved the company forward so far.

Giving the reins over is like sending your five-year-old off to her first day in kindergarten. It represents a new chapter in her life that she's ready for but deep down, you aren't.

Once early-stage startups have released their first product to market and hired a skeleton support staff, they start thinking about marketing. Usually this begins with hiring a young marketing manager to work with the sales staff.

At some point, the idea of PR is appealing – all startups want coverage in the tech press but they don't have time to actually do the grunt work of writing the press releases, pitching the news, and looking for opportunistic media opportunities.

That's when firms like ours – we are small and scrappy like the startups who hire us — step in to jump-start or reinvigorate a fledgling PR program.

Yet hiring others to work for you as employees or outside consultants never works out well if you can't give up some control. It often becomes clear fairly early on if a new client is going to micromanage or if they will let the consultants (us) do their job.

A red flag is when the CEO shares that he "knows the guys at TechCrunch, VentureBeat, etc." and that he'll work with them directly when we have a pitch.

One CEO, during our first pitch, a small funding announcement, did just that, and wound up screwing up the entire pitch by offering an exclusive to the reporter after we had already been working with several other outlets.

The star journalist didn't have time to cover the story within the CEO's timeframe, so the whole deal fell through.

And naturally, the CEO was displeased with the coverage we did achieve for him – despite a process that was too rushed from the beginning.

Sometimes trust comes through in the way executives come off during planning meetings. They don't listen to input, express unrealistic expectations for results, and even berate their direct reports in front of others.

One CEO loved to hash over the needling details, perhaps in an effort to show that we somehow messed up. He raised a stink about wanting us to correct a meaningless spelling error in an article mentioning his firm. We resisted, because it wasn't worth ruffling the reporter's feathers.

Another time, he backed out of a speaking opportunity because the coordinator wasn't as responsive as he would have liked.

Execs who need to be coddled are usually not leaders who demand respect. It seemed that there was no decision we could make without this guy disagreeing.

Other clients seem unable to grasp that their marketing lingo doesn't make for good stories. These are smart people, many of whom have founded previous companies or held executive roles at well-known tech firms. Yet taking advice from outsiders is not easy – even when they're paying for it.

The payoff of trust
Happily, we've also worked with many clients that do trust their staff and consultants implicitly. That makes for an entirely different and much more positive experience. One

startup client even trusted an intern to run the marketing department.

This fresh-out-of-college young man – we'll call him Calvin – walked into his job and working with us with eyes wide open. From day one, Calvin admitted that he didn't know a lot about PR, and was looking to us for our expertise in determining the right messages, audiences and news items that the firm should chase down.

Calvin was hampered by the limitations of a small company with lots of irons in the fire. We had many common goals for PR and marketing, but Calvin couldn't always get cooperation from those inside the company.

What was remarkable about this individual though, was his extreme professionalism. He had a direct line to the CEO and would make him available for us whenever it was necessary. He preferred to write his own press releases, but let us edit them to death when needed. He thanked us profusely for everything we did.

It's been several years since we started working with Calvin, and we have seen him grow into a savvy and polished marketing professional who wears many hats. Clearly, the CEO knew what he was doing when he took a chance on that sharp and energetic intern.

And, we've been able to be productive and achieve solid results for the company, meanwhile allowing the CEO and other top execs to focus on the job that they should be doing instead of feeling the need to do ours. That is a win-win for everyone.

Another client was looking for ideas on how to grow its brand beyond product and customer news, of which it didn't have a great deal to offer. We came up with an idea of how to leverage data that they were already collecting from customers into business trend reports.

Those reports wound up delivering fantastic news hooks for reporters in a wide variety of outlets, resulting in highly successful and repeatable PR success. Clients that allow employees and partners to run with unproven ideas, turning lemons into lemonade, show how the power of trust can open many doors.

As the external PR firm, we are hired for our expertise developing content and working with media. When companies don't trust their partners, they end up wasting their money and everyone's time. They perform duplicative work and foster an environment of mistrust and frustration on all sides.

As their companies mature, great startup leaders realize they don't know it all, and they need to trust others to help in areas that are not their core expertise. This is not to say a CEO or marketing director shouldn't challenge strategies from outsiders. But if insiders can't trust the advice of partners and outside experts, they might be missing out on a huge opportunity.

Trust doesn't develop overnight, but over time and through all the little ways that we communicate with our colleagues and business partners throughout each business day. Trust requires listening, respect and intuition.

Some leaders just can't go there – but others will, with a little prodding and time. Startup executives (and their direct reports) who have a hard time with trust may also have a hard time growing and thriving. It's through the sharing of ideas and collaboration that companies can learn and grow.

CHAPTER 14

INTERVIEW WITH DARSHAN PUTTANNAIAH

Darshan Puttannaiah **is** Founder and CEO of Qwinix Technologies, a Denver-based application development and IT services provider with offices in Costa Rica, Dubai and India. He also serves on the Executive Advisory Board of TechrIoT, an Internet of Things community.

What was the vision that you had when starting Qwinix, and how close are you to achieving your initial goals?
I formed the company in 2012, and the vision was to create a technology services firm which leverages a distributed model to build high quality software. I wanted to follow the Agile cutting edge technologies and practices to build next-gen solutions. I always wanted to focus on what is next.

At the core of that is empowering people to do the right work. That is where I started, and four years into it, we are 50% there. The reality is that we will never be at 100% of the vision. I measure this by the fact that we are growing, adding more people and they need time to adjust. Some people get what we do and others fall off.

We want to give people freedom, but that doesn't always work with everyone. So we always pivot on how we manage people, projects and technologies. Also since we provide services for the client, we can't force things on them.

I think if we were really at my vision, we would be doing more bleeding edge work at clients. It all starts with the people. We want to make sure that everyone who works at this company is happy. Those are the kind of problems I like to solve. It's an interesting problem for me. How do you encourage people to collaborate and communicate more? There are tools and technologies which are enablers, but they don't solve the problems.

How do you approach hiring?

Our employees who know how we work and can evangelize and bring others in, that is the easy way to recruit people. But from a philosophy perspective, we don't look at the degrees they have but personalities and how eager are they to learn and adapt and collaborate. So important is the integrity piece of it. Are they comfortable saying things outright, and can they admit that they don't know something?

We obviously look at aptitude but also culture fit. We use a tool called Roundpeg, which helps us screen candidates early in the process. They have to answer some questions, which takes less than a minute, and shows them and us if there is a fit with who we are. It saves us a lot of time as a first step.

How do you invest in your people and why is this important to the company's success?

We give employees unlimited vacation. There is a lot of freedom to do what you want but you need to be responsible for your own time. We are focused on next gen architectures and technologies which gives people an opportunity to work on new tools and advance their careers.

We are also involved in different technology communities and sponsor events where employees can participate and contribute. If people are curious they have a great opportunity to learn. Something new we are trying is everyone who has been with us for a year gets the chance to go to one of our other offices in another country for a week. We have offices in Denver, Costa Rica, Dubai and India. That's giving them exposure to other cultures and increases collaboration and teamwork.

Has this latitude paid off in business results?

That's a good question. How do you measure employee happiness? I believe it has had a huge upside. It took a while initially to get our advisors and leaders to buy in to this. They wanted me to follow the traditional micromanagement model but I stuck to my belief and what I had learned from my job experience what not to do.

It's been a tough journey but after a couple years now it has really paid off. People are happy. Attrition is low. Employees are willing to jump in and help others and that is a huge plus. Like every company we have issues but we get through those issues as a team. These are all signs that the investment we have made in them is coming out.

How would you describe the culture at your firm and how do you maintain that over time as the startup grows and evolves?

Whatever we do is we trust and empower people who work for us. How do you scale that? As you scale up you start introducing hierarchy. When that kicks in things start to fall down. People who started the company don't want to have access to the new people.

We hope we can create 25-person groups within the company that are self-sustaining from every aspect including HR and everything. If you go beyond that, you start losing track of the first names of everyone and the culture declines. We are at 120 people today. So how do you create the groups? That is hard. Everything new comes with a challenge.

CHAPTER 15

THE THOUGHT (LESS) LEADER

Want to see a startup CEO squirm? Ask him or her to talk about something notable that's happening in the tech world other than his product or service.

Over a combined 40 years we've worked with dozens of startup founders, CEOs and other senior execs, and the vast majority don't get thought leadership. They can't see beyond their own noses, or maybe they don't understand why they should.

Startup execs have to be laser-focused, obsessively so, in getting to market. The pressure of running and growing a company, raising money, developing product, satisfying customers, engaging media and recruiting talent is physically and mentally exhausting. It's a year-round job with no breaks.

The opportunity to create a great company is limited by the time it takes a competitor to start and grow a similar enterprise. Act quickly or else.

Marketing is one aspect of running a startup and it's incredibly important, even though founders sometimes think it's all fluff. Raising awareness for your product or service is essential to attracting customers, investors, partners, and new recruits.

The demand generation component of marketing is a company's lifeline. Companies must constantly nurture potential customers, establishing a pipeline of possible buyers and future endorsers.

In demand gen, companies can and must be self-centered. All communications, such as webinars, whitepapers and ebooks, are essentially advertisements for the company's products and services.

These "assets," as marketers like to call them, are billed as content to help customers. It's really all about the art of persuasion: which content in what sequence will most quickly and effectively deliver paying customers. To be fair, some companies do a fantastic job of creating content assets that are objective and highly educational.

PR *is about ideas and trends, not sales*

PR is much more subtle. We can't simply say: Check out our webinar and learn why our product is the best in its category. Instead, we pitch a reporter with something like: "How about a story on why cloud technology projects fail?"

We make this pitch and offer sources, such as a company, our client, whose service helps to ensure cloud implementations don't fail. We back into the pitch rather than smack people across the head with it. Reporters want stories, not product features.

The press release announcing the new product should provide context for why the product is necessary. It should also lead to a story behind the news: what does this development speak to in a grander sense? Does this new high-speed analytics tool indicate a growing demand for data in XYZ sectors?

A case study needs to focus on the customer's company and the people, not the vendor. Corporate communications is the act of delivering context for company news, whereas other marketing operations, such as demand gen or advertising, cut to the chase.

Byline articles are a great example of effective thought leadership. Over the last 10 years, print publications have been cannibalized by the Internet. As many media outlets moved their publications online in order to survive, they also struggled to keep writers on staff amid dwindling advertising revenues.

The struggles of devising profitable online publishing models continue to plague independent media to this day – with no clear answers in sight.

During this chaos, opportunities have arisen for smart people with good ideas to contribute to publications. At first you could place an article just about anywhere. Even the hottest tech pubs 10 years ago – TechCrunch, VentureBeat and GigaOm – were accepting contributed articles.

Getting a placement at these sites was a boon to a PR person and went a long way with clients.

Naturally, editors weren't pleased with this development. Yet they also knew that if they didn't accept such articles to fill their pages, the publications would go away completely. Instead of fewer jobs in editorial, there'd be none.

The compromise was that the articles had to be unbiased and not obviously self-serving. They couldn't be ads for the company or its service, and any hint that a tech product or service could solve whatever problem the article posed was likely to result in a reject from the editor.

So PR people agreed to pitch articles that didn't obviously cross the line between promotion and substance, and editors agreed to review and frequently publish said articles. The future is unclear on the market for contributed articles, but until online journalism determines a better way to fund fully staffed publications, most sites will need the outside help.

Being a thought leader means being creative and resourceful

Thought leadership should also exist on a company's own site – in its blog posts and whitepapers discussing the problems its products and services purport to solve along with related industry trends. These should be ideas, stories and lessons from someone who's had enough experience to deliver advice: such as the startup founder or CEO.

Social media posts should serve to send readers and customers to helpful resources, not just those on your own site, by the way. Thought leaders take the time to speak at local and national events, as time allows.

When working with executives on thought leadership ideas, we have to probe. We often ask them what they care about, why they started the business, what's important to their customers, what governments need to solve, what vendors are screwing up, what innovations are cool and why.

These are simple questions, really, and one you'd expect the leader of a startup company to be capable of sharing off the cuff, anytime.

The problem is, most startup executives still want to talk about their company, product or service. They have been programmed (perhaps by their investors and advisors) to never take off their sales hat. They are so focused on the business they're running that they fail to see the bigger picture.

Worse still, most can't see why positioning themselves as an expert in an industry has value. But of course it does.

We worked with a client not long ago who had a hard time with the concept of thought leadership. He was co-founder of a company in the IT infrastructure space. He came from a consulting background but was mostly a salesman and had no engineering background.

Despite his inexperience, his company was doing well. It may have been mostly due to his co-founder, an engineer by trade, who seemed to have a deep sense of how and why customers needed his service. And, they had stumbled on a market that was itself on a magnificent growth trajectory.

Our client, let's call him Bob, took the reins as head of marketing for a time, but soon transferred that responsibility to a long-time tech and business exec whom the company hired to help guide their fast-growing company.

Bob moved into a customer support / sales role and we didn't engage with him much. But when the new guy left to take another job, Bob returned as head of marketing.

The company didn't have much news so we were constantly pursuing byline articles. Conceptually, he understood the value and process, but he had no broader vision for the market so his ideas always came back to why his company and service were exactly what the industry needed.

Another client took the problem to new heights. He not only couldn't tell a story that didn't obviously involve his company, he became frustrated when asked to do so. Why, he wanted to know, wouldn't press want a story about his wonderful product?! And why would he possibly consider paying a PR person for anything other than the self-serving article he wanted?

Fortunately, some startups do see the bigger picture. The sharpest startup execs understand that communications is like any sales process. You can't hit customers over the head with a pitch because no one likes being hit over the head. You have to build trust and confidence by demonstrating that you've genuinely thought about the issues that matter to them. It can't just be me, me, me.

True thought leaders are usually thoughtful people, by the way. One client, the vice president of a software development company, could talk about the issues his customers faced without ever talking about the need for his solution. We worked with him on many thought leadership articles over an extended period of time. In all our communications with this person, he was respectful of the process and our time.

The point is, self-promotion only goes so far. Talk about yourself enough and no one wants to listen – not press, not your customers, and eventually, not your employees and certainly not your friends and family.

In our experience, the most successful startups don't have to talk about themselves. If they're really good, others will do the talking for them.

CHAPTER 16

TECH PR RULES TO LIVE BY

Lower your expectations

Yes, your story is great, but so are the stories of about 100 other startups churning emails through the reporter's inbox this week. Sorry, but you're not that special. Don't worry if your pitch is ignored once, twice or 20 times: keep looking for the right reporter who is covering your beat right now.

Get to the point

If your email doesn't have the main points clearly stated in the subject line and within the first two sentences, forget it. Nobody has time to wade through your lengthy introductions and meaningless small talk.

Be respectful

When and if you do get a reporter's attention, don't be cocky. Ask how you can help them, with research, data or source, rather than focusing on your message and yourself.

Research the reporter before reaching out

It will take you maybe 10 minutes to find out what the re-porter's covered recently, and what she has covered before that, and the types of stories she tends to write. Just as with an important sales call, come with a bit of knowledge about your prospect rather than treating them like one more generic target on your list. But again, don't send long, winding emails.

Don't pitch boring stuff

Startups like to write press releases about everything – from minor product updates to puffed-up partnerships. Use your blog for the lower hanging fruit and save the important, juicy stories for the media. These are unique stories from custom-ers, survey data, novel best practices or techniques in your field, or interviews with company leaders who have great sto-ries and perspectives to share.

Be responsive

When a reporter asks for something, for gosh sakes don't leave them hanging for days. They're busy, stressed, distracted and they'll quickly move on to something and someone else – and may never respond to you again. Do not, except under dire medical distress, skip an interview because "something else came up." At the very least, give the reporter notice if you must cancel the rare (and they are shockingly rare) phone interview.

Learn how to write really well, or hire someone who can

This may seem obvious, but writing skills are paramount to the job of PR. A confusing and poorly-crafted press release, email, case study or other piece of copy handed over to a reporter will probably kill that relationship in its tracks. Journalists (and marketing and agency directors) complain frequently about the subpar writing skills of entry level and mid-level PR people. Fortunately, there are plenty of resources today for honing writing skills, from online courses and seminars to books.

Be an expert in your sector

To be effective at driving publicity for a company, marketing people, PR people and executives need to be able to talk intelligently about many topics, not just their very own product or service. Take the time to stay up-to-date on industry trends. Maintaining a broad view will pay off in spades when you interact with a reporter or editor. Journalists and analysts like smart people who can provide a fresh angle or contrarian perspective.

CHAPTER 17

PERCEPTION

Brand perception is one of the most important assets of any company today. When you think of Disneyland, you think of..Magic. Nike's "Just Do It" tagline has defined the brand for decades. Starbucks is the place you go to get great coffee and hang out with friends. Uber is your click-to-ride, whenever-you-need-it car service. Virgin America is the airline for people who expect a high-grade flight experience.

A company can outsource technology, processes, facilities and even R&D – but not the brand. That must be curated, nurtured and owned for the life of the company.

Startup founders may not think or act in terms of brand experience from the very beginning of the company's journey, but they should. When we have initial meetings with a new client, we aim to understand what they want to be when they grow up.

Do they have a secret sauce and does it resonate in their market? Can they back up that secret sauce with a credible story that they will tell over and over again and deliver upon consistently?

Too often, the startup executive cannot answer this question very clearly. And, the answer, if it does come, isn't always realistic. "We think we can do better than Amazon!" Or: "Our product is going to revolutionize the way companies do XYZ." While those goals are possible, they are certainly not likely.

To drive influential PR, you've got to include specific and credible brand messaging in your pitches and press releases. You need to be thinking about those messages in every media interview, waiting for the right opportunity to share them.

Know who you are today

Startup leaders, particularly when they are founders, have a hard time being practical or realistic after they have been sweating blood, tears, weekends and zero or low pay to chase down their big idea. The prospect of the idea not succeeding beyond all expectations is anathema to the founder – and this isn't all bad.

Having a vision and passion are extremely important for the startup founder: it keeps him or her getting up every day to face a mountain of challenges.

Yet, even so, focusing in on what is viable and what will be the company's market differentiator is imperative, because every decision from that starting point should follow suit. Every milestone should bring the team one step closer to delivering upon the brand promise.

In the technology business, perception is as valuable as delivering a really great and useful product – if not more so. After all, there are plenty of highly talented engineers and cool products available for a quick download because startup costs for a software firm are so low.

As a young, unknown brand, however, you must be able to answer this question before you launch a product: how do you convince the market that you are worth a try, that what you are trying to do is a little more special than everyone else in your space? Startups need a compelling and clear story that will set them above the pack.

A former client in the web apps and SaaS consulting marketplace is one of those rare companies that knew exactly what it wanted to be in its early days and stuck with the program. Its leaders created a brand story that enabled the company to rise to the top quickly as an expert advising upon and implementing new web-based business models for large companies.

We knew that the client wouldn't be independent for long, and several years after founding, the company was acquired by a much larger consulting firm. The client was one of the first leaders in the space of cloud application implementation, and this claim to fame became its calling card in the industry.

Another client had a different problem. It was operating in a highly saturated segment of financial software – one in which there hadn't been much innovation or fresh thinking for years. Their idea was to create a product and brand story that would solve a brewing problem for companies storing customer data online with external SaaS providers.

Customer data is a prized asset, yet storing it in the cloud, the company's leaders said, was sketchy. Finance execs couldn't know for sure how the cloud provider was handling the data with proper safeguards and privacy in mind.

Not only that, it was hard to update customer data and combine it with internal databases for real-time insights. The complexity of managing two different sources of customer data – one internally and one externally – was a liability on many fronts, the company's founders said.

Instead, this startup's product would allow a company to keep its customer data stored internally, on its own servers, while outsourcing the heavy duty processing and reporting to the cloud. At first, we weren't sure about the message: this seemed a complicated approach when many companies were presumably going all in for SaaS and cloud-only systems. Yet in time we learned that this wasn't the case: in fact, the company was soon thriving with its message and strategy for its niche customer base.

The above observation about establishing a niche leads to another pivotal distinction for startups on brand positioning. Putting all of your efforts into doing one thing very well is almost always superior than trying to do several things at once and for different audiences.

Some startups spin their wheels for months or even years trying to figure out what product the market needs and which it can deliver upon successfully. To compensate for a poor strategy or conflicts among the leadership team on direction, the marketers (sometimes at the direction of the CEO) keep the company alive by changing the message:

taglines, product name and descriptions and web copy might be refreshed every few months, just to see what sticks on the wall.

This makes the job of PR people sheer hell, because we cannot tell a consistent story to the press. Worse, a constantly changing message confuses customers and market observers. One of our clients shut down because the company could not hone in on a critical need to fill its market, could not produce a workable solution, and ultimately (or even initially) never had a compelling customer message.

Another common problem is working with the sort of founders that see themselves as one thing, although the reality is something quite different. Very few startups can, within their first year in business, disrupt their market. It takes time to prove out the idea with customers, finesse it, and grow mind share.

The CEO has a vision of what the company should be, but there are usually phases in getting there. One of the worst problems for PR people is working with founders and execs who have an outsized perception of the brand today.

They don't understand why top-tier, name-brand publications and websites don't care about their pitch. They don't see the point of starting with smaller publications to get initial coverage, because they are so focused on the *Fortune*, *Wall Street Journal* or *VentureBeat* clip.

Company perceptions change over time. Being realistic while also shooting high when the opportunity arises is smart. Being humble and grateful for any press opportunities while you are just getting started indicates that you have a great attitude. Ignoring all PR opportunities except for the ones that you think are worthy of your company/ideas, is not. Sticking with a message until it is time to change, is also important.

By working with the PR and marketing team on the right brand messages and stories, ones which are realistic and credible, while also powerful, can help a fledgling startup find its way in the market faster than competitors.

CHAPTER 18

SMOKE AND MIRRORS

In PR, we sometimes start working with companies that are in the middle of a transition. This can be tricky, since one must still sell the existing products while the startup team is focused on a future that is unclear and not yet real. The CEO doesn't want to talk about what is, but what will be; yet in PR, what will be means nothing to the press.

Reporters covering technology companies don't care much until the product is on the market and in use. They want to hear from customers and they might want a beta copy. They crave numbers and real-world stories.

They don't want to hear about any product when it's in development, unless of course you are Facebook, Google, Twitter, Microsoft, Apple or Amazon. For startups that are slow to get a product in market, the initial PR strategy requires creativity – and patience.

We worked with an infrastructure software company that had been given a new breath of life by an investor entrepreneur who bought out the family founders. The company was barely surviving, and the legacy product was dated and of limited interest to new prospects. The new team came in with an idea to reinvent the company with a brand-new product.

"It was the Holy Grail, a software-defined platform that could work with any hardware on the market and give customers a single pane of glass view into their infrastructure," the company's former marketing director told us, after she had left the company.

This was exciting stuff, since midsize and large companies spend millions of dollars integrating and managing different components such as servers, routers, storage appliances, monitoring tools, security systems and more. It's a complex and entangled mix of technologies that must work together seamlessly, and be managed around-the-clock, to avoid major errors and outages that affect users.

The company's new CEO and startup team felt they were onto something big – something that could be a real disruptor in the IT industry. The product would be a silver bullet, making infrastructure management much easier for corporate IT managers.

Unfortunately, the CEO was almost invisible to us. Occasionally he would jump on a call, but didn't seem to have much to say. It turns out that he didn't have a solid grasp on the market opportunity for the new product. He failed to get into the weeds of the new platform as it was being built.

Then, two weeks before an important trade show, the management team learned that the product was significantly behind schedule and would not be ready to demo at the show.

The reality that was playing out for company leaders at the time couldn't have been less than horrifying, as the former marketing chief recounted: "There was no cohesive platform nor thought process to go from zero to this huge platform. For a short time we thought we could revamp the legacy product, but then we shelved that idea as well. Worse, we knew that the legacy product was past its prime. It was five years old and couldn't scale."

Many months later, the engineering team completed a piece of the platform that had potential, and the CEO tried to sell it to a large high-tech company. Yet this effort as well fell through at the 11th hour. The CEO had no other choice but to lay off employees and begin the process of shutting down the business.

As the external PR resource, we knew nothing about any of this behind-the-scenes drama. When things were looking extremely dire for the company, we were under the impression that the product was receiving its final touches. Nothing could have been further from the truth.

Finally, Kevin received a call from the marketing director explaining what had transpired and her plans to leave; we were surprised yet not shocked. There was too much information withheld all along, and the lack of a viable product to pitch after more than a year had left a sour taste in our mouths.

"We were figuring this out on the fly and there was no strategic decision-making going on at all," said the marketing director. "We were in a situation in which we needed someone who could step in and be a strong leader. The CEO had done this many times before over the course of a very successful career, but at this point he wasn't up for it. Failing fast is important, but we didn't do that. We should have seen the signs and reset much more quickly before we started to run out of money."

Lessons from the field

Our work as the PR team for this client over the course of two years had been a series of fits and starts. The product was launching soon; the product would launch in six months. We want to focus on this message; actually, now we are focusing on something quite different.

When you're on the outside, it's impossible to know the real truth. We saw the signs that this company was not moving forward in a positive trajectory, yet we could only rely on what the marketing director was telling us during our regular calls. It certainly wasn't her fault: she had to keep the information internal as everything was exploding around her.

In a case like this, what is PR to do? You get scrappy. With no news to the deliver nor case studies and events to promote, we turned to thought leadership. Despite the challenges, we were able to secure several bylined articles by the company's executives on topics related to their target market.

PR teams must often make lemonade out of lemons. We don't always have much material to create pitches, and while we would never recommend masking the truth, it is always important to place a client in the most positive light possible.

Some PR people can deal with this; others will run for the door. In our case, we developed a great relationship with the former marketing director. She's now moved on to another exciting adventure, and still believes in the value of PR.

"Many startups don't hire marketing or PR for a long time, which is a mistake," she said. "I think PR is a critical element because nobody knows who you are as an early stage company. PR is the first real driver of building awareness for startups."

We couldn't agree more.

Conclusion

Startup Life

When we set out to write this book, we wondered if our opinions would be valuable. After all, we know nothing about creating a tech product – only publicizing it and explaining it clearly to others.

But once we started putting words on the page, we became excited – not just about the prospect of publishing a book, but about the fact that we were writing about innovators.

Most people, whether they admit it or not, have had a startup dream of some type. Americans are, by default, dreamers. We all want to make our mark somehow on the world, and making good or great money while doing it is better than, well... you fill in the blanks.

It takes remarkable courage to launch a startup. There is the fear of failure, fear of making do on a negligible income for many months, fear of judgment and there's even fear of success. What does it look like if a company really does take off, and now you're at the helm and you must lead the troops forward?

As small business owners ourselves, we know what those fears are like. There are months when income is low and when clients never seem to be happy enough.

You worry that you will have to go out and look for a "real job," where you have stability and corporate perks, but far less control of your destiny. But then suddenly, luck turns and there are more clients than you can handle.

Life is good, and it's crazier than you imagined and you're just dog tired, all over again. Then one day you wake up and realize: Wait a second, I think I kind of like this roller coaster.

For all the creators, inventors and those who fund and support them, we dedicate this book to you.

www.ingramcontent.com/pod-product-compliance
Lightning Source LLC
Chambersburg PA
CBHW051722170526
45167CB00002B/759